First printing & online edition 2020 by
Mayflower Publishing.
110 Rantoul Street Beverly, MA 01915

www.marshallsterman.com

PROCEEDS

All proceeds from the sale of this book and its future versions shall be contributed to The SeedLink Foundation.

The SeedLink Project, founded in 2015 by tech entrepreneur & angel investor Tan Kabra (www.tkabra.com), builds interlinked eco-communities across developing nations, providing micro-financing, critical resources, and housing exclusively for local entrepreneurs and their families.

After completing a successful small pilot program, the SeedLink Foundation is now in the process of establishing it's first three 500-unit eco-entrepreneur villages, evenly spread across 2,000 miles.

Entrepreneurs accepted to live in the SeedLink villages receive a small business loan which they repay towards their local SeedLink Fund to better the community, educate, and fund the next wave of young entrepreneurs. They must also relocate their entire family within the compound and purchase ANY and ALL goods, materials, and services from their fellow resident entrepreneurs. Village compounds are spread distanced strategically so that those who live in the communities in between can still benefit from all the burgeoning trade while SeedLink works hard to expand rapidly.

At the current rate of admission and adoption, SeedLink expects to have over 3,000 units across 5 village compounds by the end of 2021.

To learn more, visit www.seedlinkproject.com

FOREWORD

My "Random Walk" is a narrative of my thoughts and stated opinions from the early Obama years as chronicled in my many "Letters to Editors", Tweets, Face Book posts, and E-mails to "Friends". Using these "platforms", I voiced my doubts and concerns with the decisions being made by our elected and self-anointed savants. Foremost among their activities was the destructive Bernanke "bail-out" which did away with due process, picked winners, and altered our previous terms of business engagement-by writing large treasury checks rather than sending out bankruptcy notices. As you might expect, this book is a regurgitation of those thoughts, opinions, positions, and prejudices from then till 2014, perhaps casting some doubt as to the rational of its content, since opinion is in the eye of the beholder and time does pass.

While we all watched as this played out, one thing remained the same- my love affair with entrepreneurs and my never-ending search for capital for their basic needs. God bless them, because in most instances they, their families, friends, and especially their investors, knew not what they were in for.

It's also quite a challenge to make a substantive case for my expertise in view of the fact the reader today has access to a decade or so of my prognostications and proclivities at a time when there were very few high batting averages. Because of this, I plead Nolo. My net worth suggests I'm no savant, but I am a glutton for punishment, and am hell bent on stating my case, standing my ground, and staying in the game, no matter how you score my card. My objective, as always, is to seduce "sophisticated investors" as I need their capital to help me jump-start, or add some more fuel to the tank, of one of the many new opportunities I continue to fall in love with.

The title for my journey was stolen from HBS classmate Burton Malkiel's "Random Walk Down Wall Street". It concluded that stock markets were inefficient, i.e., not addressable scientifically, and thus represented an unpredictable randomness. I believe my title is fitting, and there's many an early stage investor of mine who can attest to that fact.

I'm a product of a coastal town, Beverly, Massachusetts, so insular that when I go over our bridge to Witch City Salem, I'm concerned I'll be missing some action at the Italian Community Center or our Gloria Chain Store. But I'm lucky being here in that I'm a stone's throw from Cambridge and numerous colleges, universities, VC's, and start-up "Labs", which provide more than enough dreams of others that are ripe for my harvesting. That said, my ultimate objective is to package a few of them by way of the public markets as I await a call from Joe and Becky asking me to become a CNBC Squawk Box Contributor- my dream of redemption and resurrection.

I've also come to understand, after a 60 plus year search for Ten Baggah's, that even some "luck" is not a "gimme", and one needs more than skin to play the game. Getting up and taking a few more swings is the only way I know to be part of it, knowing full well that The Invisible Hand is a huge factor in the ultimate score; one might even get lucky by getting hit by a pitched ball and forcing in the winning run. In any event, make sure you have a bat in hand even as your being sent to the showers.

My advice to those who want to follow my yellow brick road is to start by getting a bit part in the chorus line, and then trying to go solo in the world of your choice. For me that universe was in finance, funding start-ups and early stage tech companies by placing bets on entrepreneurs, who are also attempting to build their field of dreams in challenging, competitive and changing landscapes. They too are armed with less than a full tool box; but then again, no one else has one. In this world you are fortunate, or lucky if you will, to be more right than wrong, as the latter outcome generally destroys hard won business and personal relationships.

In my world there are no crystal balls, nor is anyone omnipotent; forecasts are often by-products of an overzealous imagination and are as often as not plagued or detonated by unforeseen, un-predictable, future events. Accept the foregoing as Gospel; the odds of picking winners at inception, or even during incubation, elude the best of handicappers. Business building from the ground floor up, as is the case in a random walk, has yet to be reduced to a winning formula. Contrary to what our VC's in academia are preaching, and in spite of the many labs and hot spots for entrepreneurs in training, there's no prescription for the early stage vertigo that comes almost without exception; it's art, not science- see how long you can stay airborne without revenue, never mind negative cash flow.

After Beverly High '49, Brandeis '53, the B School '55, and four years in the Navy improving my gin rummy game and third base play, I managed a small specialty manufacturing business for three years before opting for straight commissions, hawking what was then a relatively new investment product, mutual funds, for Burbank & Co, a one office Boston stock broker. During the day I cold-called every business, legal, medical and dental office within 25 miles of Boston, while at night I was on the phone with anyone who had a pulse and didn't hang up immediately. I built a "book", which included some extraordinary business, accounting and legal mavens, and soon became infected and afflicted with their insights and aspirations.

Once I was more fully aware of the value of what they were chasing, I was bitten by the bug and opted to "keep score", an objective never suggested by my professors. In today's world that course of action has become an addiction, not so much for the lucre, but for a place in the winner's circle. You'll hear more about this when I discuss today's Entrepreneur's Cult and the fantasy-land approbation given it by those who should know better. That includes those leading the charge at The B School, who for some reason have passed the baton to the local VC community, resulting in aborting the curriculum that made my alma mater in the first place (How soon they forget!).

An inevitable next step led me to the investment banking side of the brokerage business. This introduced me to my first love, financing early stage companies via the public markets. In 1962 I became one of 3 founders of Markoff, Sterman & Gowell and the Merry Go Round that ensued for the next 50 plus years became both my pride and joy and often-times my burial ground. The fact is that throughout that journey, and even to this day, I still seek capital for start-ups and early stage companies, many in which I play multiple roles. My intent is to help entrepreneurs pursue their passion by getting them funding from investors who are looking for home runs; funny thing is, at no time along the way would I have described it that way.

My investors are usually friends and family, clients of small brokerage firms, family offices, money managers, and a vast array of "sophisticated investors", paradoxically referred to as "Angels" (in SEC parlance they're "Accredited"). In the 60's they were looking for the next Polaroid; then in order, IBM, Xerox, Apple, Facebook, and lately, anything that Marc Andreessen blesses, or what our more sophisticated, and soon to be disappointed money mavens refer to as Unicorns. My mission was to deliver out-sized returns by selecting, pricing, and structuring investments in early stage entities, and then escorting them to the next round of buyers, whether through still another private round, an IPO, or a "reverse" merger into a public entity, the objective being to provide an "exit" or liquidity option, so that the pied piper in me could enrich and expand my investor base in anticipation of my next high wire act.

The script was always the same, a business plan with a proforma that predicts rising revenues, cash flows and profits, as well as a companion set of boiler-plate risks which are rarely fully read/appreciated and/or once identified, can be dismissed because the company is singularly 'unique'. Today's plat-du-jour is a "Deck", a slide-show presentation that is designed to excite and captivate even the most incredulous in the audience. It's a business plan on steroids that conjures up the largest future value one can imagine. The business plan we used in the

'60's through the late 80's has been abandoned as it doesn't leave enough to the imagination and is too much work to decipher.

No matter the pitch, as a Wall Street War Veteran with enough imbedded shrapnel to sink the Titanic, and one still intent on surviving the carnage from his "next best thing", I still need (as others do that tread this path) investors/believers who can endure the pain (RISK) that comes with the territory, and not insist on retribution (my scalp) if the script leads to unintended consequences. I do know one thing for sure, you cannot get directors for a public company unless you have Board insurance, a fetching monthly stipend and annual stock options. So, what does that tell you?

Harvard's Shikha Ghost concluded that about 75% of all start-ups fail to return anything to their initial investors, which is the reason that the most repeated words in all offering documents are the RISK FACTORS (Note the traditional bold print). It is also the reason that investors need to be SOPHISTICATED and/or ACCREDITED. Despite these warnings, investors armed with cadres of high-priced attorneys, reread their Offering Documents only after their dreams of outsized returns are shattered and then look to me (individually) as a port in the storm. As you might imagine, and a fact to which I can personally attest, immediately after the first negative report to shareholders, there are no more high-fives, and I'm crossed off still another dance card. I also need to change country clubs, stay away from family events, seek new friends, and abandon charitable pledges. As the 'intermediary', guess who's responsible for losses? Gains on the other hand have nothing to do with the pied-piper and everything to do with the brilliance of the check-writer.

While it might have only been me, I viewed myself as a merchant banking professional who worked to deliver outsized returns to those who trusted my judgment. Given the no-growth years after the demise of Lehman and the closed windows of the banks to those in need, it may be that I was the only one that had that opinion. I absolve and/or delude myself, by pointing out that this past decade has been a high wire act for any performer. Not only did one have to deal with the financial melt-down and subsequent investor disconnect, but our Fed induced market comeback favored the blue-chips and/or anyone with a huge market cap, and not the likes of my up and comers.

In my sand box we also had to deal with the built-in bias of our regulators (both governmental and industry related) who directed our citizens to casino's and lotteries as opposed to low cap IPO's and early stage Private Placements. This behavior penalized and crushed micro-cap companies, notwithstanding the preponderance of evidence that this sector fueled our historic economic expansion and had been a bonanza for VC's, Angels and a legion of small investors, who by the way, pay taxes, purchase goods and services, and reinvest after tax profits in a continuing cycle that also added jobs- a multiplier effect that has been sorely missing.

There is no official score card chronicling my efforts, but in retrospect, and factoring in the very difficult recent years where "marks to the market" (non-public valuations) far outnumbered "liquidity events", I believe that both my batting and slugging averages in what is euphemistically called "Alternative Investments", placed me behind Silicon Valley's highest quartile, but well ahead of the Thundering Herd's. That doesn't mean that I can now come out of the cold without fault, as there are many victims of my overarching enthusiasm, but the bruises are fading, the jury is still out, and I see a light at the end of the tunnel for a few stragglers. Having said this, and with arthritic fingers crossed, I still pray they don't extend the Statute of Limitations.

Despite a decade of class warfare in which our regulators sentenced early stage start-ups to purgatory, I remain hopeful that we will return, even with the full implementation of Dodd Frank, to a past when open markets, not biased rule makers, enable entrepreneurs and other risk takers an early-stage market option. Let's reset the tone and truly jump start our economy by going back to the system that created the jobs that led to a better way of life for most of those willing to work hard, make sacrifices and participate in the struggle Our politicians and those entrusted to carry out their mandates (sweetheart deals for their constituents) play a significant role in making the necessary bargains to produce this kind of change; so what's the chance they'll make decisions which result in prosperity for the many, not just the few?

My point is that we need a regulatory re-engineering by those who control the flow of federal capital. The historic creators of 2/3rds of new jobs (the entrepreneurs who are the first to put new shovels in the ground) need to access capital from investors who can evaluate risk in a pro-capitalistic economy and do not have to look for additional help from our Fed and our electorate. History has shown that those who put their money where their mouth is have a far better chance of picking winners than those not subject to personal risk, and who can pass on loses to tax payers as a matter of course.

I also want to talk about entrepreneurs and jockeys and the fact that they don't walk on water (individually and as a species) and certainly don't look nor act alike and cannot be reproduced in-masse as the Harvard Business School would have one believe. Truth be told, those that dare to tread this lonely path need more luck than skill, by far the biggest impediment to predictability. I base this on years of experience (pain) and is recounted in later paragraphs which contain a litany of complaints about the species from their friends and family, who out of necessity both fund and live with their aberrant behavior. You'll see that our poster child is a breed that is not easily categorizable and conjures up descriptions that run the gamut that includes "intractable" to "unreasonable". Two things are certain, they're not easy to tolerate, and you won't find them taking a play day off.

Along the way you'll also get an earful of what's truly important to life, limb and happiness as you assess the investment opportunities that you are presented with. No need to go into details here, as A) it may result in you putting this tract aside, or B) you will have my secret sauce and no further need to listen to the pied piper. Towards the end of my soliloquy you'll find some of my "Letters to the Editor", to "Friends", and some Tweets. They're included to show you my state of mind lo this past decade - what I was thinking, reading, listening to, and my suggested remedies regarding the economic and societal events that caused a great divide. They also give these musings a heftier feel, and let my grandchildren know that their Ippy/Pop Pop can do more than tell them to put down their iPhones and stop texting when we're together. - *Marshall Sterman*

CHAPTER 1

I overheard a conversation between four former government appointees discussing their new career moves after six years of working together, during which time they determined the flow of capital and well-being of a significant portion of U.S citizenry- the "they" being Ben Bernanke, Tim Geithner, Larry Summers and Bob Rubin. In God They Trusted, as we in them, and Believe It or Not, they've graduated from working for the masses and are now being rewarded by the Wall Street crowd they benefited so handsomely.

The emasculation of a once vibrant IPO market for early stage and micro-cap companies has taken place over the past twenty plus years under the radar (except for those victimized) by the investment banking and venture community, which had a vested interest in dulling/eliminating this activity. They were aided and abetted by the combination of industry, Federal, and State regulators who thought they were protecting the public by winnowing out the smaller brokerage firms, along with the consultants, legal and accounting professionals who supplied capital and succor to start-up and early stage companies. It was accomplished by pricing second and third tier players out of the market by slashing commissions and fees and greatly inflating regulatory and other professional costs associated with the process. These regulatory guardians of our capitalistic society acted more like the Gestapo, rather than protectors of our "rules of the road", as in, this is what the law calls for.

This attrition via regulatory burden was further compounded by financial industry trade associations and exchanges that allegedly represented all the players in the system but instead prostituted themselves to the bulge bracket firms that soon became "too big to fail". Adding insult to injury, while "We the People" have paid the price, the "Masters of the Universe" were somehow exempt from punishment; no heads rolled, and token retribution extracted, not from The Perpetrators, but from the coffers of their clueless, non- conspiratorial shareholders. And while the electorate have been given some scalps of secondary players, the lucre of the market will not change behavior (some would say "character"). It will, however, increase the use of hand signals and winks while limiting and e-mails and telephone calls. It certainly will not lessen the bidding at Sotheby's or home prices in the Hamptons and on Nantucket.

The bias that has crippled what used to be a source of capital for the start-ups and early stage job creators, and the havoc that this loss has wrought, had nothing to do with fraudulent behavior, whether by the penny stock scammers or the scheming of the Enron's, the Arthur Anderson's or almost everyone of size in the mutual fund or investment banking/brokerage community. Likewise, Sarbanes Oxley, while a poster boy for over-reaction and so called "unintended consequences", was a contributor, not the culprit.

It's a simple case of economics; both price and "rule" the little guy out of the marketplace and you own the space yourself, or at least until the margins you're enjoying are too mouthwatering for others to ignore. It's a tribute to capitalism that the rewards, though far more difficult to obtain, still drive, motivate, embolden entrepreneurs, investors and markets to adjust and adapt, no matter the pain, to these adverse changes. These days it's called 'pivoting'. Many are now abandoning their series of brokerage licenses, leaving the registered brokerage firms (SEC oversight) and turning themselves into junior Bain's, (Gretchen Morgenstern refers to it as "Private Equity's Free Pass). How sweet it must be to double bill your investors. No wonder I'm on AMTRAK and not the New York Shuttle.

The challenge to those without names like Goldman, Fidelity, Black Rock, and Morgan, is simply to survive and live to fight another day (life springs eternal- as does the material quest). This drive to smell the roses has created hybrids - the reverse merger, the convertible "bridge", the PIPE, the SPAC, and a regrouping and realignment of past competitors. Technology generally triumphs, and the Bulletin and Message Boards, along with a multitude of day traders, have carved out additional market space that cannot be controlled by the wire houses and their institutional cohorts. This is especially true of the new internet "platforms" that are essentially (at least for the near-term) information disseminators that broadcast to the ends of the earth and, until lately, have not been recognized as worthy of competitive shelf space. This too will change as those with will and technology forge their way into the honey bucket. What stronger motivation than this to get an invitation to an Allen & Co. confab at Telluride?

While these one-offs gained some respect and brought limited relief to still far too few, Face Book came to an abortive rescue (thank God for it's not-to-late comeback). As a poster boy, it brought notoriety to pre-IPO investors outside the traditional conventional players (the West Coast sophisticated investor celeb list where only the 1% of the 1% need apply). Good intentions being the breeding ground for subversive activity, the idea of the privileged IPO gained traction, so for awhile it looked like the "unsophisticated" 99% would continue to be fleeced by those that deemed them unworthy of venture investing and only fit for Keno, Lottery, Scratch tickets and Casino's, most all of which were conveniently located only a stone's throw from public transportation, schools, coffee shops and soup kitchens; and all soon to be joined by a new breed of bootlegger, the marijuana dispensaries.

Help appeared on the way when Obama's Crowd Funding initiative seemed to resonate with what appeared to be well-intentioned regulators. But alas, recalling broken promises in the past, the SEC made sure that Crowd Funding was Dead-on-Arrival, while at the same time allowing our politicians to continue to trade on insider information. One might call this a hat trick or trifecta; for me it's par for the course.

So, who really cared at the time? It was just another 'miss' for a job starved economy where entrepreneurs abound with tin cups in front of an impenetrable regulatory wall (think of them as "Way off Wall Street"). In the old days this treatment was referred to as being "shafted". Now you know why the small Broker-Dealers are either gone or a non-factor. They were neutered by the Big Boys and their regulatory counterparts, as well as the other legitimate source for funds- remember what banks used to do? They've posted "Out to Lunch" signs on their front doors ever since we bailed them out, whereupon we then compounded our error by providing "stimulus" and then "quantitative easing," instead of prescribing an enema. Both Mr. Frank and Mr. Dodd have made sure that this bias will keep the 1% free and clear of all guilt and having future impediments to their continuing financial well-being. There's plenty of shame to go around because this need not to have been the case. Keep reading to get through "Marshall's Plan", a job creator that could have helped get us out of the batter's box and on to score.

But maybe I've spoken too quickly and with too much cynicism; there's some talk about resurrecting old fashioned Reg. A's and the possibility of using them as auditions and tryouts for the great white way. There's a faint promise that they might pave the way for early stage company's accessing the world market for funds, thus enabling even a handful of them to truly make a difference in the lives of many.

It may not be fair, but we're allotted just so much time to figure things out and make decisions whose consequences we have to live with, while the Invisible Hand writes and the market's Random Walk continues. Risk, Opportunity, Security, and Safety are in the eye of the beholder. At times there is no obvious choice, many paths to follow, and a greater divergence of opinion as witnessed daily when Steve Liesman and Rick Santelli , Carl Ichan and Bill Ackman have a go at it. At the end of the day you pays your money and you takes your chances; surely Goodness and Mercy............

On my agenda, which ties into the recently defined Reg. A, is to fund a brokerage firm that does one thing only, online IPO's. I have not checked with the SEC's enforcement arm, but my sense is that this is now a possibility as long as it is "fully compliant". The thought takes me back some 55 years when Sterman & Gowell, generated at least twenty-five such offerings without the benefit of a vibrant internet that's a voice for all who have something special to say. I cannot understand why the Wolves of Wall Street (there are quite a few still stalking our public marketplaces) haven't recognized this opportunity. They should be beating this drum, generating conversations on Face Book, and Tweeting its virtues. It could fill a huge gap in small cap funding without the fraudster implications being used to slow the Crowd Funding death march. The early stage "unwashed" should be hoisting the flag and saluting Best Efforts Reg. A's, while looking for attorneys, accountants and investment professionals that can guide them through this less-threatening voyage.

The most important aspect of this journey is COMPLIANCE- making sure that you are in lockstep with both the SEC rule book and the considerable individual Blue Sky requirements. It's challenging and a "Must", but it isn't insurmountable. You need competent council (as always), and an accounting firm which qualifies for public company representation (PCOAB certified). As an "Issuer" (the IPO candidate) you are also responsible for all filings, including individual state Blue Sky requirements. Having gone through this drill many, many times, and being fully aware of the sweat, tears and costs involved, my vote is still in favor of the process because the many advantages that the public market offers far outweighs what are minor costs when the proverbial bell is rung and your investors have an option of going to the cash register on any trading day.

As part of the compliance package the underwriter and/or issuer, needs to be certain (verify) that his investors are who they claim to be, and that there is nothing in their background that deems them unfit to buy and/or own the offered securities. A Best Efforts Reg. A can be offered as a self-underwriting by the Issuer, or by a broker/underwriter and/or syndicator. In every instance the investor's money is held in an escrow account before a 'closing'. If the IPO is not declared "Effective" (i.e., the amount of money required was not met, or the underwriter has new information which makes him decide not to "close"), the escrowed money is returned to investors.

What makes this a viable option for both the Issuer and the underwriter is that many of the prohibitive costs that are now killing public raises for underwritings of under $10M are pared substantially under a Crowd Funding format. Under this scenario the underwriter (if he so chooses) does not have the burden of the overhead associated with office costs and brokers, as well as the sizable percentages paid them as part of the allowable commissions. Best Efforts offerings have significantly less stringent capital requirements, as there is no need for capital to buy shares from the issuer on the closing date if buyers fail to pay for their orders.

Best Efforts and Reg. A's were always available but the brokerage firms that might avail themselves of such an option were hampered by their "reach", i.e., their investor base was limited. In the 'good old days' (pre-social media, etc.) both 'white shoe' and boiler-room operations were burdened by the regulatory requirement to pass along information via one-on-one telephone calls to clients, the lack of large managed accounts, and the need to rely on underwriting materials (disclosure, etc.) sent via mail and overnight delivery. On the Issuer's side, there is the virtual elimination of the excessive costs of road shows, additional travel, entertainment and the need to pick up breakfast, lunch and dinner for brokers who had little idea or intention of "selling" the issue to clients, or to using the IPO to get new accounts. It was a free lunch or dinner with cohorts while the impoverished CEO's maxed out their personal credit cards.

The most important protective element in any underwriting remains the same- Full Disclosure, i.e. information that the SEC deems necessary for an investor to make an informed investment decision. That's the reason the process takes time. Our regulators, rightly so, have to make sure that the filing, the IPO itself, measures up to criteria long accepted as warranted and reasonable. That shouldn't change; investors need to be apprised of Risk Factors, financials, the cap table, officers, directors, advisors, professionals, a business description, marketing plan, competition, assets (intangible and otherwise), use of proceeds, and a host of other information that the company, its professionals, and the regulators feel is necessary for investor protection. All this needs to be tempered, without puffery and promise. I'd prefer to see the 'simple language" which was supposedly adopted some 20 years ago. As long as the investor has had an opportunity to read all that our regulators, the Issuer and underwriters deem important, and the Issuer can pick up a certified check at the end of the day-- "mission accomplished."

CHAPTER 2

Who you listen to and what decisions you make are more important than one can imagine- hindsight being a plague without an antidote. You and your loved ones will either prosper or suffer consequences that have to do with what you choose not to do. Sometimes it's a coin toss and you'll never know when you lucked out.

So how do we pick from the cats, dogs and vast array of thoroughbreds seeking funding, while holding off the herd and their insatiable and insane drive to prove that theirs is the greatest idea, the biggest opportunity, the new way to save the planet? How does the proverbial WE (me and thee) get to a "Yes", or even a "Maybe"? Malcolm Gladwell's "Blink" provides the answer. "Like pornography, you know it when you see it". You also know that everyone has some form of astigmatism and you have to hedge your bets by playing more than a few opportunities. A diversified portfolio with my "product" is what I think is in the investor's best interest as long as it's his Vegas money. Going for the fences makes for great cocktail conversation but generally poor batting averages. You cannot win the lottery without a ticket and there are plenty of "I shoud'a, could'a, would'a" stories, but then again, that's why there are so few Roll's and River House's.

What's my line-up? Who do I send to the plate? What do I need to know to make these choices? Don't forget, in the Early Stage League we're dealing with rookies and over-the-hill veterans. We're not in the Majors but winning by getting a return on investment that dwarfs the averages is still what this game is about. Without early round draft choices (for which you pay handsomely) one is forced to cobble a band of irregulars, fund their activity, and fashion a squad that could return more net profits from smaller gate receipts and the sale of hot dogs and beer than any of the opposition's overpaid, underperforming big leaguers. You'll also have to get used to a recently adopted VC phrase that is used to bandage the usual injuries. It's called "pivoting" and obviously is an excuse for failure and the need for a new game plan, i.e., a way to continue hustling your investors with fodder that covers prior mistakes and transgressions and might, just might, now prove to be a winning combination. It's like being at the slots and using tonight's taxi fare to make sure you continue to play before the next guy hits the jackpot while you are at the ATM.

My choices, those investments I lust after, generally have many other investment banking options. After all, I'm not the only one seeking the hand of the fair maiden. Will she accept me for what I am? ...agree with my view of life hereafter? ...accept my term sheet? Will she agree with my use of proceeds, the make-up of the Board, and my ability to access the public markets for the next raise, etc. ad infinitum? If the entrepreneur and those he listens to don't buy into my script, the file goes into the green plastic trash bag I put out in front of the house every Thursday morning, and we start with the proverbial blank page. It's probably for the best, since dialing for dollars is not the easiest nor most admired work. Remember I'm not a V.C; I come with love, not money; or more precisely, consider my two hashtags, "Carpe Diem" and "Godfather".

One of the biggest keys to success is being able to identify and work with the brokers, attorneys, accountants, research boutiques, and IR/PR firms who can still "deliver" in this space. Nothing is a slam-dunk, especially when you have to uncover investment opportunities with an unranked management team that you have told investors will create near term liquidity in/within three years- easily said, tough to deliver- with outsized returns tied to that timeline. You must also buy into management's ability to use the funds to get to a valuation that's needed to justify the risk. And unless there's a significant improvement in our overall economy- which I am not forecasting- I have probably understated the timeline to investors by anywhere from 2-4 years. So if you join the early stage investor parade, be prepared to be a long term investor, amass a file of "Letters to Stockholders" to memorialize a variety of annual excuses, and budget accordingly while you hear me repeat the oft sounding excuse and old saw that "you cannot win the lottery without buying a ticket".

CHAPTER 3

My favorite movies are Casablanca, True Grit, Pretty Woman and Shane. So how the hell have I wound up with the cast of characters I have had to count on to shape my legacy? What's it all about Alfie?, might be a better question to ask. I've been in a shotgun marriage with an element in society which defies description, as in no two are alike. Many are just plain smart, while others are grinders with a mission. No twins but plenty of knock-offs; I try and stay away from the "Certifiable's". As always, "The Difficult I'll Do Right Now. The Impossible Will Take a Little While." Or perhaps it's just "I Did It My Way"

I've finally 'come out' and am admitting to a long, lasting, love affair with entrepreneurs (jockeys) and risk takers (investors) no matter their age, infamy, or infirmity. It's not that I'd like to be dating them per se, nor am I a closet voyeur. I have been cohabitating towards a shared, common goal- getting into the winner's circle. And it's not for the roses. The 'purse' can be significant, especially when you've monetized your piece of the pie via the public markets.

For the most part I don't blow them kisses nor tweet their daily actions, but salute my entrepreneurs by standing in the front row and cheering them on. They've played a significant/meaningful role in transforming our country into its position of dominance and leadership. But entrepreneurs are only part of the picture; they might put us in the Red Zone, but we need more than a good quarterback to score. And isn't that what's it's all about for everyone involved. It's truly a team effort.

While they're the jockeys, the designated stars, there needs to be a 'band of brothers', a team comprised of a multitude of supporting actors that aren't necessarily motivated by similar objectives. I'll take that back; everyone in the pool wants to make a buck and/or show others that they are smarter, more important, and a key factor in making something big happen. Over the years the make-up of this menagerie has changed, as well as the leverage they bring to the table in their particular roles. The "regulator" has replaced the robber baron, not in itself a bad thing, but the outcome for the entrepreneur, the risk taker, the creator of the opportunity, has a less likely chance to succeed in getting what he needs in order to get to the finish line unless the numerous unintended impediments to progress are overcome. In plain language, the pendulum has shifted into an area of prejudice which bodes ill for early stage development activity and action. The guys with the badges (and unfortunately some prejudices) oftentimes think they are paid to keep the status quo, no matter how it negatively impacts the changes needed for a vibrant, expanding future economy.

There were/are some government agencies (thank our lucky stars) that understood the need to succor/encourage this activity; DARPA and the likes of the In-Cu-Tel's, to name just two. We also have to lay a wreath at General Georges Doriot's bier and acknowledge the contribution (for me it's grudgingly) of the VC and Angel community who both recognized that you could profit greatly from betting on the right jockey, team, and/or technology in a start-up or early stage company. But that supportive cast is also having its problems, some of its own making, but most having to do with two main themes that have done most of the damage to the structural integrity of our employment engine- the attitude and mandate of our regulatory agencies (both governmental and industry self-imposed) and the over-compensated, preening, self-congratulatory masters of the universe (our investment and commercial bankers) who have profited from the protection afforded them by forcing the adoption of "off-limits" licenses (talk about non-compete licenses handed out by the use of treasury bail-out money). Theirs is an unholy marriage where the participants are as comfortable in DC as in NYC. Pardon the digression but more on this later; which doesn't mean that I am suggesting that there is a formula, prescription, mandate, and/or guarantee of success.

While many entrepreneurs have been rewarded, I'd wager that the human toll- as measured in their living standard and the impact of their activity on other individuals (family members, investors, employees and advisors) has resulted in emotional, psychological and economic harm far more devastating than the material gains of the combatants. The personal "cost" is unfathomable and, if truth be told, the many outstanding colleges and universities that trumpet the virtues of the entrepreneurial bent need to tone down their rhetoric or set up psychological triage centers for graduates who bought the lemonade but couldn't peddle it. I salute Babson and its complicit cadre of academic strongholds that trumpet the entrepreneurial spirit, as if it were a religion that rewards its adherents. Unfortunately, and I repeat for the second time, HBS has genuflected as an idolater to the siren call of Silicon Valley- 'will it and they will come'. Better that these neophytes get gainful employment and some business experience before entering a world that you need a lot of firepower to navigate in; talk about amateurs vs. pros.

And still another take by me; entrepreneurs are now on the A List, particularly if they have a Palo Alto address. Steve Jobs has upstaged Gable, Bogie, and Eastwood, while Zuckerberg is a cinch to win his second Emmy. But for the most part, you'll find the preponderance of entrepreneurs in either Chorus Line or

Annie. They're competing for 'discovery' and have bought into the fiction that 'The sun will come up in the morning''. In reality, each story line is somewhat different with an abridged version starring almost nightly on ABC's Shark Tank, which continues to circumvent the usury laws to the glee of an expanding audience. In fact, we're seeing prostitution on a scale that's been taken to another level. I know- "Jealousy will get me nowhere."

An entrepreneur's affliction/curse comes with rules and regulations that one doesn't generally equate with a Democratic Capitalistic System. A major contributor to any early stage wannabe is the danger from unwarranted and unrequited regulation, most of it a result of the overpaid ex-pols who then funnel campaign contributions and other emoluments to our lawmakers, who then pass legislation favorable to those who can afford to pay for it, rather than on legislation that favors job creation and opening the gates of opportunity for the entrepreneur/innovator. Look around; who, if any, have stepped to the plate? Aside from stock buybacks, mega acquisitions, increased dividends, and salaries and bonuses which trickle down to a modest extent, what has been done to move the employment needle? I am not discussing the pros and cons of a $15 per hour minimum wage which in time will come, but if mandated rather than competitively induced, will prove a job killer.

Except for those who are seeking highly prized skill, few if any in the Fortune 500 deserves a gold star for their contribution on the jobs front, even though they were the first to benefit from the Fed's gluttonous stimulus, which unfortunately was force fed at an immeasurable cost borne by most of our working and unemployed. As a lame excuse, we've been constantly reminded that those with IRA's, mutual funds and other related equities benefited from the market move, forgetting that the bulk of lower and middle income accounts are in savings banks, not much help in this no interest environment. Funny thing though, and a little known "fact", our Congressional credit union has a mandated guaranteed 12% annual interest rate with the guarantee that no annual record being sent to the IRS (just kidding). If anyone can get it both ways you know who that is.

With the economy still in the outhouse (how else would you describe today's conditions) it's the dead start-up, pre-revenue, early stage entrants (many still figments of their creator's imagination) that slog it out, hang in there (no new clothes for the kids) and try and make a difference. That takes real guts. Compare their courage (stupidity?) to our insulated corporate leaders who, with billions tucked away in overseas accounts, opt out for share buybacks and more pruning instead of investing for both the company's and the Good-Old-US of A's future growth. Oh, I forgot, they have to also keep enough ransom money to assuage the regulators and the likes of our activist luminaries, most of whom have replaced Willie Sutton in going after what's in the vault. Next thing you know Carl Icahn will be on The Blacklist with his sights set on Paul Krugman. My bet is that when warmer weather comes around, we'll see much better organized tent city occupants. Their ranks will be swelled yet again by the graduates of our great institutions who cannot find work, and if so, cannot cover basic needs and college debt repayment. What they should concentrate on this time around, is changing U.S. law so that they can discharge their debt the same way everyone else does. Hello, Detroit? Chicago? …. never mind Greece.

I need to be careful I don't run away with this by getting into a debate about the self- interest of "the corporation" or its responsibility to whom and to what? But let's stay away from passing judgment as to "character", morality, legal and possibly ethical issues. We eventually come out of the cave for food, not love. In today's world that means we're interested in lucre, stash, bitcoin, moolah, green. "After me", shouts the guy or gal atop the pyramid. What's more basic than wanting more than just preservation? I guess that's why entrepreneurs are fighters first and lovers last, still another trait that contributes to their well above average divorce rate.

Recognizing and accepting this as "normal", and appreciating that wealth in itself should not bring prejudicial consequences to those fortunate enough to pursue and then gain from the fruits of it, the Barbarian's at the gate are ever preying, so that enough fertilizer needs to be spread as soon as possible in order to promote some sense of fairness to those who may or may not deserve to taste the honey; or as my Zada used to say, "the good and welfare" (or did he mean "the good on welfare?"). Unless something is done about this before the millennials need Viagra, the most important app on your Apple watch is the call for your protection from any of the 99% who resent the 1%. The reason the pyramids were built were not for the mortuaries they turned out to be, but as safe havens for those who thought they had to protect themselves from the maddening crowd. This is why Richard Branson and Elon Musk are so interested in getting out of this world and their manifests are sold out.

CHAPTER 4

My Bubba used the Yiddish "chazeri" to describe my teenage "mishugus". This comes to mind when I use the Lord's name in vain by referencing the Ten Commandments. Ditto as I set forth my proclivities. If Bubba used an English term it would have been "bull-shit". I didn't come down the mount with tablets, but I've had plenty of time to give penance and will once again take the opportunity in this confessional to seek forgiveness for my numerous transgressions. Beyond that I'm hoping there's good karma and a "legacy" for the benefit of the many that comes out of my musings. As my dad used to say, "Write when you get work."

Rather than bore you with a mind numbing TEN COMMANDMENTS, I only have EIGHT. Their relative importance is ranked in descending order and comprise the list of my decision making imperatives/ attributes as to the investment characteristics I lust after. Prior to my fully 'coming out', I want to make a point about entrepreneurs, or the so called jockeys most VC's, private equity and Angels parade out when pitching investments to their own investors. Quite frankly, they are only #4 on my priority list. Simply put, while it doesn't necessarily mean that you will never get to the finish line because the entrepreneur/jock leaves his fly open, you want to make sure beforehand that you can replace the guy when you feel necessary, i.e., make sure you have the votes to do so, as well as a Plan B which gives everyone an additional shot on goal, the meaning of which is that with tools and tenacity you can do a complete about-face, reorg, and/or restructuring.

Pivoting is not enough. It allows you to calm down your investors by putting lipstick on the pig; but for not for long. Before your investors wake up to the pain of a mental write-off, your investment banking competitors will have tweeted the ambulance chasers, a la KKR's and Blackstone's investments in the oil patch. To put it into perspective, why would you continue to ride in coach when you can upgrade to a premium membership on Net Jets?

While I devote a great deal of time to talking about the people I usually fall in love with, you will miss the point of the entire exercise (making money by taking risk) if you do not accept my first three postulates, none of which has to do with leadership, i.e. those we have defined (at times incorrectly) as entrepreneurs. So, here's my VIII Commandments in descending order of importance.

#1. A VALUATION I CAN FEEL GOOD ABOUT - The most important consideration in any investment (whether real or sweat equity) is to be rewarded (paid) for risk. It's a very simple concept. Money in the bank, U.S treasuries, and collateralized loans, while seemingly risk free, are not on my dance card. I'm all about risking a portion of your funds so you can be very well rewarded for bucking the odds.

Valuation or "pricing" has everything to do with what I believe the company will be worth after handing management the baton and making sure they have the time to execute their game plan. It also has to be comparable to what I can defend as 'equal risks' versus other alternative investments. My first responsibility is to my investors, not the insiders who have agree to follow my game plan, so I rarely see eye to eye with those insiders on valuation. Besides, if they need me, what does that say about their options, and why not press my advantage for my investors?

The vision of the founders is set forth in the Company's Business Plan. The further out it goes (5 year revenue and profit projections are de rigueur) - the less you can count on its accuracy. In structuring better returns for investors versus others, you tie management and previous investors to those projections. I reward them for making their numbers and penalize them (reward/protect investors) when the fourth and fifth year projections fall short. Always remember what Murphy said, the odds are heavily weighted in favor of the "unknown" and unexpected. It's a law. Every plan, every implied promise of victory, is only a starting point, and it's always related to yesterday, very rarely tomorrow. If you could hold management's feet to the fire by having their equity track their forecasts, the chances are that you'd leave them with a paycheck and little else.

Nonetheless you need a starting point. It's always the case of me wanting more for my investors, and management wanting more for themselves. Who could have guessed? My preference is to test the real market by dialing for dollars. At the end of the day, it's really a question of what an investor needs to receive in order to close, and most likely that's a full meal and not the main dish. As you may recall, our playing field has few real competitors and time can take the shine out of a contestant's smile. So I get to throw in resets, warrants, convertible features, the proverbial kitchen sink for my investors.

If you use my Shark Tank analogy, you'll appreciate that for the most part, ne, in almost all cases, the deck is stacked against the entrepreneur holding the tin cup and expressing unrivalled passion; it's essentially a rigged race to the bottom. When you have the cash, the means to someone else's end, and also infinite time versus the seller's constant tick tock, the advantage is obvious;

supply is endless, there's no lack of fodder, and "them that has the gold" reel in them that hasn't. If the entrepreneur cannot cast a wider net he'll never be indistinguishable from the pack; achieving value in the early stage marketplace requires a machete not a pocket knife.

#2. A TECHNOLOGY/PRODUCT THAT ADDRESSES A LARGE AND EXPANDING MARKET - No matter what the product/concept/service is, we don't want to invest in anything that needs to capture a large part of a market to get a handsome return; nor should anyone else. And even if we were lucky enough to tap into the mother lode, unless we had a lock on that market because of I.P or some other quirk of nature, we would be exiting long before our original business plan called for, as we would then get higher selling multiples than originally targeted and be "taken out" as others anticipate future sustainable growth (which is rare).

Almost all business plans assume the world as their market, and then tell you how easily they can get 1-2% penetration; which, if they gave it a second thought, would make them the most profitable company that anyone has ever been fortunate enough to have an opportunity to invest in. That market is always huge and includes the kitchen sink. But the fact is that market size is not really important, except to the extent that investors buy into it. What's important is 'traction'; someone is actually paying for your product or service. Now you can make a case for extrapolation (multiply that 1%-2% identifiable market by projected margins that are still figments of management's best guesstimate) and hope that the 'greater fool theory' will bail you out. Call it what you will, while we aren't entranced by market size at the outset, others are mesmerized when revenue begins to have the faint outline of a hockey stick.

#3. MARGINS YOU CAN DRIVE A TRUCK THROUGH - Margins are more important to survival than market size. Show me a company that can make a lot of mistakes and keep its doors open and I'll show you a company that will reward its investors. Unfortunately, Early Stage companies rarely meet their projections; man-sized margins disappear in practice, costs are generally underestimated, and revenues most often inflated. The bottom line is that, in almost all cases, in order for margins to materialize and give us a shot at liquidity, we will need additional financing- read- 'other believers.' This is why #4, "Articulate Management", is vital.

For the record, when revenues begin to ramp up, management violates the margins they originally projected, first by both undercharging out of fear of losing a sale, and then not having the courage to reduce spending. They're boarding the Delta Shuttle to LaGuardia, instead of taking AMTRAC to Penn

Station. I keep telling my Jockey's- the market will forgive losses in early years and will overpay for a company that can earn a buck early; but that advice usually falls on deaf ears. Put another way, once you give most entrepreneurs their money, your advice is no longer heeded.

#4. THE ENTREPRENEUR, WHO IS AT BEST AN ARTICULATE SPOKESPERSON AND CAN HANDLE THE CEO'S ROLE - I look upon them as my "Jockey". Angel investors and VC's have deified the position so that potential follow-on investors will genuflect and be cued up for the next round. I think of them as necessary "bait", but in-spite of that insight, I still fall in love too easily. Alas, I am only human and dismiss too casually the multiple pitfalls that should have curbed much repeated ill-fated enthusiasm.

You'll also note that I have not said that "I bet on the Jockey". If that is what investment success is all about, you might as well have a resume contest. The problem is that these guys are just not easily handicapped in spite of their most recent performance. Yesterday's jackpot winner may never cash another ticket. He's also not as hungry or the 'workaholic' one needs, and is now enjoying an asset laced portfolio and country club membership. I guess what I really want to impress upon you is that when you manage in the minors (my playground) you are not picking from the top draft choices; but then again, you are not saddled with their salaries, perks and benefits.

While their experience and exploits are drawing cards, I've learned over the many decades that you should try to recognize 'staying power' and 'flash in the pan' successes, qualities not apparent in a resume. You live with your choices, warts and all, and figure you'll need to turn a second stringer into a starter by imparting wisdom while you cheerlead and handhold throughout all the expected trials and tribulations. Most important is that you make sure you have a good Board of Directors and advisors who have some skin in the game. The truth is that these kind of 'insiders' are harder to find than those you entrust the key to the front door to.

I'm also going to tell you right up front that I haven't a clue as to which jockey might be best in any given situation. Even Red Pollard blew a significant lead in the late stretch on Seabiscuit. You can only ID a winner after the fact. The same guy that hit it out of the park yesterday, dropped an easy fly ball for a loss today. There's simply no DNA or Rorschach test for this one.

Aside from doing the heavy lifting (no mean feat in itself), if your Jock cannot excite the crowd, then it's a much more difficult Run for the Roses. My job is to put them on their mount, genuflect when appropriate, and hope they can cast the spell necessary to get money rounds A, B, and C accomplished at ever increasing valuations. I don't need an Emmy winning performance, just a nomination equivalent. Remember, getting the funds to execute, even the least meritorious offering, is the goal. The #1 order of the day is to get the money. Give me a candidate more akin to a Barrymore than a Valentino. Why do you think the electrician is more important than the lead singer? It's the sound effects!

While I hesitate to use the word "promoter", a reasonable facsimile that makes you believe his efforts are transformational, is my candidate. If you don't hear that your guy is "fabulous" after a presentation, maybe even out of the ordinary, then you're in trouble. He has to wow investors. VC's sell themselves to their investors and can suit-up another candidate at will. I'm stuck with the date I brought to the dance for the entire road show and ever mindful that I might have to put on a tear stained straight face and say, "I'm sorry it didn't work out pal but there's a more important role you can play", and still manage to stay afloat until the next 'pretty woman' is bedded.

Lest I forget, my Jock has to recognize from the git-go that, although he's getting star billing, he has to share the goodies/upside ($$$) with promoters, consultants, and a host of bit players who get the clapping started and warm up the audience. He must also understand and appreciate the need for investor liquidity and an initial valuation that allows investors to reap some of the rewards. This is what guys like me have to get across to hard working, totally committed, under-funded, out on the edge founders who have maxed out their mother-in-law's credit cards and don't have the next tuition payment for their brightest. I have several speeches for this, each one requiring the American flag and a handkerchief.

Without exception, as I've explained some paragraphs past, my jocks are "soiled", which for the most part is good because they earned it and in so doing passed through the gates of hell and are still standing; it's the #1 trait I look for. It's called working-stiff experience and you cannot teach it. This experience also puts them at a disadvantage when the equity goodies are passed around and it's my job to see that they are treated fairly if they remain on the first team. They're willing to be tested by the Derby but you don't want them hiding in the barn when you need them out of the gate at the Belmont. Six furlongs is a cakewalk; a mile and a half can wipe one out.

They also understand that they cannot even suit up for the VC's, and that therefore there's a limited market for their services, i.e., they are not in the best position to negotiate. So, while I have a great deal of empathy for Jocks in general, I am too familiar with the odds of success, the hurt of failure, and the need to maximize returns for my investors. If you cannot meet the mortgage payments on Park Place you're off to the Burbs. I assuage these less than noble attributes by appreciating the fact that the successful jocks will soon leave my nest and jump in bed with someone who wears a new suit, well fitted suit, or has a Sandhill Road address.

On the other hand, it's an advantage if your Jock is unemotional and somewhat heartless (none are initially programmed this way). Think for a moment of what they have to deal with. They are piloting a virtual start-up; truly early stage. They have to make choices between family and saving my rear end (not a good example because the choice here is too easy but…). Mother wants him home, he needs to get a regular paycheck, the kids need attention, the lawn needs mowing, his in-laws have been merciless and wonder why their daughter doesn't pack up and leave. Tell me, do you want the good guy who is responsible to family, puts them before the business, and hands you back the keys, or do you want a son of a bitch who says "Sorry dear, you and the kinder are moving in with your folks"?

I'm jaded. Experience has taught me that I'll be mistaken, ne taken, by many of my entrepreneur/jockeys. I don't mean that they are dishonest or disingenuous, but they do what they need to do for their dream to continue. Accepting this as reality, I probably should be more diligent in my own due diligence (a longer wooing period), giving me a chance to consider whether the honeymoon will last longer than the time it takes them to clear the investor's funds and take control of the check book.

Still another verity is that my Jocks will never be nominated for "Entrepreneur of the Year". This is good news- it makes for low ball initial valuations which in turn gives me a shot of raising money from more knowledgeable investors (this is my #1 reason for doing a deal). Also, even though you are led to believe it, no one from the VC community or the hallowed halls of academia has come up with a formula for "Keepers", or an easy "Pass-Fail" test for start-up CEO's. So while I don't get the pick of the litter (DNA is always suspect anyway), my initial CEO expense is minimal, upkeep is substantially less, and I get to pick the attorneys, accountants and the rest of the cast. Writer-director- producer-distributor-ticket taker: what's not to like?

Point of fact; no kid in a hoodie need apply. Make that anyone under thirty-eight years of age unless accompanied by friends and family or a benefactor who will put up the needed seed money. And they'll be no exceptions made for the hordes of Harvard Business School grads who have opted to drink the cool-aid; i.e., dedicate the next four or so years of their life to rampant entrepreneurship (opting out of a real job) and pursue a passion that a professor helps you fashion. WTF, do they actually believe that entrepreneurs can be created a la Henry Ford? Perhaps, but that's contrary to the data out of the University of California, Berkeley whose research concluded that the average age of tech start-up founders who have successfully raised venture capital is thirty-eight, have a Master's Degree, and more importantly have 16 years of work experience. One out of three (using the HBS model) just won't cut it; $$ FUNDING $$ is a necessity. Investment bank WR Hambrecht uses algorithms when they handicap investments and their conclusion is that the founder, the entrepreneur, in most cases my jockey, represents a mere 12% factor in predicting success. This buttresses my conclusion that a lot of HBS, Babson and Stanford grads will be in breadlines before their fifth reunion. My recommendation is that, for those that meet that fate, their student loans be forgiven and they get a free pass for another two years that includes room, board, babysitting, alimony, and psychiatric treatment.

What my jocks also need to have (and the whole cast if possible) is skin-in-the-game. I want everyone to feel the pain if they fail. Purple Hearts are O.K, but I want to see friends and family suffer if my investors have to take a 'hit'. In addition, I need marathoners, not sprinters. This is an Iron Man competition. It tests grit and determination, and when it really comes down to it, "STAYING POWER". As long as they never say "Uncle" we'll find a way to right the ship. How can I ask someone to wager on our thoroughbred if our jock stops whipping in the stretch?

I also need a workaholic who will fight with me at the onset of the dating game with respect to valuation, terms, presentation, etc. The guys that roll-over are either wimps or they are so afraid they won't be funded they'll say or do anything to get a pay day. I need a slugger who will rev up still another time AFTER we decide what direction is right for the company. This means that he recognizes that THE company come first and "giving way" to others who may be needed to get the company to that next level. My role is do whatever it takes and whatever means are necessary in delivering the oxygen, while prepared to do battle with anyone who gets in our way. If you think I'm inept in playing the Game of Thrones best to look for a youthful Dorian Gray or get a referral from the likes of a Steve Schwartzman.

While Jocks come in all sizes, shapes and personalities, embedded in their DNA is a will to win and an overriding (though oftentimes masked) contempt for naysayer's, and an unflinching belief in their own eventual success. Unfortunately, they also think the finish line is earlier in the stretch, but as long as we go to the cashier's window everyone will be happy.

I also like and respect a Jockey who will fight for what he wants and doesn't get personal. Unfortunately, that's not a quality you can determine from the outset of the relationship. Most of my money raises take time and involve others in the syndication process, so there's plenty of stress and second guessing for everyone. It's like a round of golf; at the end of 18 holes you know all about your foursome; their character, personality, likes, dislikes, and foibles. Most importantly, you also know whether you want them to be in your next foursome; which is one of the many reasons I enjoy Joe Kernen and am addicted to CNBC's Squawk Box. Joe truly appreciates that aspect of the game. At the end of the day "Character" is what it's all about.

Truth be told, after I'm "All In" (the check's been cashed), I'm not always happy with my guy's leadership, nor is he with my advice (this creates a particularly strident relationship when his story line changes, and his milestones are missed). Since it can get too destructive if one goes to the Board or one of its members, I prefer to stay in touch with my maverick, make challenging or threatening observations, avoid discussing "differences", and hope to improve our relationship over time. I'm not being a 'traitor', but I need to keep the lines of communication open with management, so I am still in a position to possibly change the dynamic, and also able keep investors apprised of what is happening. I also try and get out of the way by bringing in a "replacement" to develop the rapport and relationship that I couldn't achieve. It isn't about ego; it's about staying alive and coming close and/or exceeding our targeted return. I'm all for opportunity, but not for entitlement. While everyone deserves their appearance at the plate, getting around the bases isn't a Right; you need to get on first, FIRST. That's where attitude, will, determination and skill come in. And if you need to get hit by a pitched ball, take one for the team.

#5 PATENTS/INTELLECTUAL PROPERTY OR FIRST TO MARKET ADVANTAGE - I don't subscribe to the value generally attributable to patents, nor do I believe that first to market is that important. Both are selling points to investors and help create an "exit" option. Call it sex appeal and window-dressing. Why do I believe this is a fact? Think about it, if IP is so valuable why don't banks lend against it? You very rarely have to give the entrepreneur value for it as neither will your V.C competition. However, if you have been lucky and stumble upon a true "Platform Company"- IP is it's essential element and I'd have to value it far up on my list. I also know that I won't be invited to be part of a discussion on the matter by VC participants, so I've left it at #5.

#6 INFRASTRUTURE/COPRORATE INVESTMENT NIL - While it may seem trivial by contrast to the other elements of the deal, I want a relatively small organization that is barely appropriate for the size and timeline (exit) anticipated by the investment. There's no way my investors can carry an operation that household VC's and investment bankers take on. Having said that, the truth is that you always (yes, always) need more money, and when things become extremis (an event detrimental to my investors- unplanned, unfunded, unable to be coped with from existing resources), my CEO must be able to send the workforce home for some unpaid vacation time. Survival is a must and having to make lease and rent payments, support unproductive machinery, and pay bills unrelated to ongoing revenues is simply not an option. With no time outs left, the game clock winding down, and no defibrillator in sight, all extra weight goes out the hatch. So why have it in the first place?

#7 POSITIVE CASH FLOW WITHIN 18 MONTHS - Sure, we all want to get to positive cash flow and it generally takes longer than 18 months no matter the pro-forma. But that's not the point. I need a plan that demonstrates we can get there. Of course, it has to make sense and is reasonably achievable. I need this for the same reasons that buttress my infrastructure analogy. This means you stay away from early-stage biotech and pharma even though they're relatively easy to raise initial capital for. There's no way to stop the cash drain. For a host of reasons which have to do with the care and feeding of scientists who generally have big ego's, short work days, and the need to take expensive trips to stay au-currant, unless your war chest is bursting at the seams or you have a sugar daddy, you'll never stop panhandling. You're also taking on the 'have's' in Big Pharma and the FDA who both have a long history of defending the status quo. Better to focus on those opportunities which require far less money to get to the market; or at least you believe this to be the case.

Because the odds are that you won't get to where your pro-forma says you will be on schedule, there's generally a need for others to pick up the necessary follow-on financing, so start the process of finding that source well before you have to lift up your skirt and drop your draws. The difference with being miles away from cash flow or being able to say that "it's just around the corner", is sometimes the difference between keeping the lights on, or filing Chapter 11. Keep in mind that while we can live with the "Beast" if we have to, the next guy will always opt for "Beauty" and stay away from your bedroom. A little cosmetic surgery can make the difference between getting funding or pad-locking the place. Let me err on the "almost there" as opposed to having to admit that "profitability is a long way off". I'd rather have a product ready for a low-cost infomercial than have my guys cooling their heels in Bentonville, hoping for shelf space in Fargo.

Let me repeat, the Holy Grail is positive cash flow. Most start-ups never get there, and if they do get close, panhandling is not an option since you've already gone down that road. If your team doesn't deliver to the point at which your funding was geared (which is more than likely the case), you'd better be able to execute Plan B, which allows you to change direction ("pivot") so you keep the lights on until you regain enough stature to either create income or an illusion that allows you to access more funds. Revenues demonstrate that your product is attractive to someone in the marketplace; someone is actually spending money to pay for what you are offering. I know it's a difficult concept (especially to those that never had to meet a payroll) but the primary objective of business, or should be, is to create revenue, while everything else is to support this effort. Believe it or not, profit is not a swear word. For my investors the quest is to 'value' that business in whatever part of the cycle you find it, structure and price for the new reality, and then pray like hell.

#8 AGREEMENT AS TO EXIT STRATEGY - While there is never a formal agreement, nor in any event could you hold a management that controls the Board to it, you need to talk about exit almost at the same time as you lay out plans for seed capital. In fact, I believe that there's an unsaid/implied pledge to your investors that their shares will one day trade publicly. They should have an option to make their own decisions re selling, especially if the company is doing well and is growing and the value is recognized in the public markets, while at the same time their personal agenda is enjoy and secure their gains, and take their own victory lap. It's one thing to have the option of liquidity; it's another to be stuck with a lifestyle management that believes that staying private is for their personal pleasure and privilege. I have heard more jockey's using Sarbanes Oxley as an excuse for staying away from a possible liquidity event even though they have no idea of what that law is all about. There should be a stipulation that CEO's sign which binds them from Day 1 to a 'filing' (IPO or other public market option). Investors are entitled to that exit no matter the valuation or venue. If I cannot in all honesty and with conviction tell an investor that the Board and CEO are committed to listing on a public market if and when successful, his response for our investment request should be, "I'd love your deal, but all my investable funds are committed."

Now that you have my #1 through #8, you need to know there is an overarching fact that even I must acknowledge; my "children" will never win a beauty contest. Even if they are only "cute" I'll never get to adopt them. So you'll know ahead of time; you will never be investing in what others might describe as a "wonderful company", a great opportunity. There's no Cinderella on our team, not even a Snow White. I am a bottom fisherman in a world that eulogizes fly casters. Remember 'the eye of the beholder'? We shop on-line, not

Bergdorf's. We're also early sellers (our time horizon is anywhere from six months (bridges) to 18 months (IPO's or #144's). Talk to the pro's in Silicon Valley, Shanghai, London or Hong Kong, they'll tell you there's no need to "go public"; plenty of private capital to get you there and plenty of time to harvest the fruits of your investment a decade or so down the line, while at the same time they're deducting their 2% while you're tapping your withdrawing from your 401K to make ends meet. It's just the way things are today, as always: A.K.A. death and taxes. My steadfast rule is that you overpay when you expect to wear the same suit to weddings and bar-mitzvahs, but when you need something for a one night stand there's no need for cashmere: translation- 'he who respects tomorrow will increase his chance to truly enjoy the fruits of his labor. Don't overplay a winning hand, and always pocket spare change as you rake in the big pots. There's plenty of 'action' but you need a ticket that's always tied to a payout.

CHAPTER 5

Con artists have a lot in common with investment bankers; I could say the same for "tort lawyers" who partner-up with their clients by charging 25%-40% of any recovery from the ship wrecks that ran aground from willful misconduct. There's also a big buck to be gleaned by exposing illicit activity by the likes of 60 Minutes, CNBC and a parade of "Hosts" showcasing the colorful Willie Sutton's nightly. What this has to do with my discussion about an "edge" and coming on a playing field that is already mine ridden by earlier rounds is simply, you can easily be sucker- punched by a variety of resets (re-pricings) that greatly reduces your upside. My guess is that many later stage investments in most all of the Unicorns will result in disgruntled investors whose returns, if at all, will pale versus those whose bankers had insisted on preferred returns.

The attraction of the Alternative Investing Game is that YOU, the guy that may be able to get the fair maiden off the run-way, are the "House". You get to shuffle, deal, and enjoy an edge, as in "Those that have the Gold make the rules". It's true: "money talks and bull shit walks". The dealer gets to Structure and to Value. Your offers are often rejected or renegotiated, but the fact is that this is where the rubber meets the road. Remember, it's you who picks the beauty pageant winner and can send everyone else home. Make sure you spend quality time with your own people- attys/accts/those with experience and insight you trust to give you their thoughts about deal terms. You might be a great artist but now's the time to see what someone else's brush strokes look like.

What I strive for is to lock in/reach for return, defined as what you, as my investor, might receive/get back from the bits and pieces we opt for. Valuation is obviously important, but upside is oftentimes more a function of structure. Who said that the extra warrants were throw-ins? We kill for those 'incidentals'. Let me repeat- STRUCTURE OVER EVERYTHING ELSE! I'd rather have a smaller slice of the pie if it comes with lots of toppings and a few extra cookies (collateral, puts, resets, preference returns, discounts from future market prices, etc. etc.).

To put it more simply: what I crave for my investors is one of the following:

1) "Bridge Loan with Kickers": This is simply a term loan with a stated interest rate and a "kicker", defined as an additional opportunity for return. Usually the kicker is composed of a convertible feature, common stock and/or warrants. I build in one or two rollover periods which allow the borrower to extend the loan's maturity by giving up additional equity

and increasing the interest rate during the roll-over period. Rarely is the borrower able to pay his first maturity date, so rather than not anticipate this and price it ahead of time, you plan for it to happen and up your return substantially. When your tenant gives you the call and tells you he'd rather sleep than you, you can yawn and have pleasant dreams. Keep in mind- always- if the borrower needs you, his pro-forma is only slightly better than a start-up's, and 2), "Performance Based Equity Giveback": There's always a tug of war when it comes to valuation. Guess who thinks the company is worth more, the investor or the entrepreneur? Almost without exception I give the entrepreneur his valuation (take the price of the shares you purchase and multiply by the total shares outstanding to get to that valuation- using that formula you get the additional value of what you invested). Additional protection for my investors is built in since the valuation is tied to the business plan pro-forma. A "miss" rings the redistribution gong since it's a given that management will never meet their projections, which means that the giveback provision will increase the percent ownership of current shareholders (my investors). This translates into a higher percentage ownership at the expense of the original insiders.

By accepting the original terms, but insisting on this repricing reset, we also lessen the chance of losing out on a good deal going elsewhere. Pricing/valuation is not a science, but you can take a lot of the guesswork and negotiating out of the equation if you can agree at the start to forecasts that force management to base their valuation/pricing on, If that valuation is in line with what is then the "generally acceptable" market rational, we raise our hands and hit the bid. This way a lot of the guesswork is taken out of the equation and my investors have a re-pricing put (All's fair in love and war!)

We could also add a Reset or Discount to a Future Market Price but I'm getting way into the weeds. So let's get to the advent of the PIPE. It is a "have your cake and eat it" approach to investing- we can have it both ways. My investor's money comes with an innocuous proviso; it is packaged in some sort of convertible that "can convert at THE LESSER OF, a given price per share or at a certain discount to the market at the time of conversion. Think about it; as long as there is a trading market the investor has to make money on this investment. Also think TOXIC because that became the fate of many of our dear departed. Crystal ballers simply "re-set" to whatever price allows losers to work out of their investment (the assumption being that there is a market even for the ugliest children), or they were prescient, and shorted when any opportunity arose. For the most part we need shed no tears for these enlightened investors who truly hedged their bets.

3. "Royalty/Convertible Play": You don't see this used very often, but it's a way of getting liquidity for investors while keeping an option open for getting another bite at the apple. The only kind of company that this is effective with is one where the fixed costs are in place and margins are in the stratosphere: we don't want a people intense business as overhead is a bad word. You better be right and get to traction quickly if you have these imbedded costs. The convertible feature is a necessity in that it gives some exit options (maturity date, IPO, sale). This is part of the original structuring and is 'priced' so that it doesn't cap the potential return for investors.

We'll also be trying to negotiate for any and all of the liquidity options noted below:

A. The sale or partnering with a portion of the ongoing cash flow going to my investors

B. Payback or maturity of debt instruments

C. Royalty payments to shareholders tied to product sales

D. IPO or 'reverse' into a publicly trading company

E. File for public company status and then do "shelf" offering

F. Sale of position to another investor/private equity fund

CHAPTER 6

While I still have the stage, I want to add my two cents by siding with those who felt that the first TARP was one too many. If that weren't the case, why are those that were engaged in the deception still defending their actions? They all appear to be on the same side of the political spectrum, figuring that more of the same thinking makes for a better solution.

I disagree with the accolades heaped upon the saviors of our banking system who continue to say/believe that they averted us from another decade of the '30's. What they did do was to triage their buddies, tranquilize the rest of us, and deep-sixed the un-annointed. I'd rather treat the few with cancer, no matter the consequences, than to drug the many so they are walking dead for who knows how long. Certainly the Feds haven't figured it out as I write this. But why beat a dead horse. Is there something that we can do today (NOW) to get Uncle Sammy his mojo back? – I hope you understand that I wouldn't have asked if I didn't think I had the "solution", or a reasonable facsimile.

You also know how I feel about the early stage start-up ethos and the cast of characters and world beaters who inhabit that ethos. There's no antidote once you've been infected, unless you've struck out more than a few times and are forced into early retirement. But, for the moment, let me cross the aisle and talk about the single most important by-product of start-up/ early stage enterprise from a broader perspective; they create jobs; and much more. In the no-interest world we live in today that's been a boon created by the Fed for the bankers and brokers. There's no way they can also play the role of the enabler, the jump-starter, the alchemist that opens the gates which have locked out the able bodied that are ready, willing and able to create the jobs of the future if only given the enabling platform. If any 'borders' are open, these are them!

It's been a long time coming, but there's a hint of recognition of the dirty little secret behind the generational change that has crippled many of our early stage, micro-cap companies despite the fact that this sector had been a bonanza for VC's, private equity, angel and public investors in the distant past as they fueled our historic economic expansion.

Let's finally admit that the emasculation and erosion of this once vibrant market place has taken place over the past twenty years and has been in stealth mode except for those who have been victimized by commercial and regulatory assassins. It was scripted and sponsored by the investment banking and venture community who had a vested interest in eliminating this relatively small and certainly non-life-threatening activity. The Masters of the Universe were aided and abetted by the regulators who winnowed out the smaller brokerage firms, consultants, and the legal and accounting professionals who were necessary as hand maidens in the capital chain that gave life to these job generators.

This 'winnowing' was accomplished by pricing second and third tier players out of the market by slashing commissions and fees for small cap public offerings, trading in decimals, and greatly inflating the professional costs associated with the process. Furthermore, this attrition was compounded by the industry trade associations and exchanges that should have been representing everyone in the system instead of pandering to the bulge bracket firms who were the same ones that ultimately became "too big to fail"; and by the way, whose leaders were somehow exempt from personal accountability. No individual punishment; fines (if and when) came out of the pockets of their underrepresented and non-conspiratorial shareholders. If shareholders were duly compensated many ex-corporate officers would now be housed by the government instead of their beleaguered shareholders.

On this subject we now have an abled body expert witness, Neil Barofsky, the guy who policed the $770B (yes folks, the "B" is for $Billion$) Troubled Asset Relief Program ("TARP"). He uncovered the dirty little secret, which he aptly refers to as "regulatory capture". The banks, the too big to fail investment houses (Lehman was not a member), and many governmental agency (Fannie and Freddy come to mind) were in protective custody. Domestic pets were neutered while jungle predators where let out of their cages.

This bias and the havoc it wrought in the early stage equity arena had nothing to do with fraudulent behavior, whether by the penny stock scammers or the machinations of the Enron's, the Arthur Anderson's or almost everyone of size in the mutual fund or investment banking or brokerage community. Sarbanes Oxley, while a model for over-reaction and the undisputed "unintended consequences" poster child, was not the main culprit, although certainly a contributor. It's a simple case of economics; price the little guy out of the marketplace and you own the space yourself, or at least until the margins you're enjoying are too mouth-watering for others to ignore. It's a tribute to capitalism that the rewards, though far more difficult to obtain, still drive/motivate/embolden entrepreneurs, investors and markets as they adjust and adapt, no matter the pain, to these adverse changes.

We need a new paradigm for the SEC to endorse. It's painfully obvious, one size doesn't fit all, especially when "He who has the gold" dictates. Being able to write the check is what it's all about. Only in that respect is it an equal opportunity playing field. Don't show up without "green" or you'll be fouled out. You pay, you play. There's no need for the regulators to protect these guys from one another; the truth be told, they look out for one another. You can't tell me that Barclay's wasn't aided and abetted by Chase, ABN and the Thundering Herd in establishing our overnight Libor rates. Proceeds from the fines will add to the employment rolls at the regulatory agencies without perceivable benefit to anyone else; shareholders will shoulder the costs, and bank execs will be less than forthcoming at congressional hearings.

Truth be told, regulators (SEC, FINRA), our anointed protectors, smother the weak and the defenseless, defined by me as anyone who cannot afford attorneys with offices in buildings with more than two stories. As ump's, our regulators are "homers" for the bulge bracket firms. They are totally and shamelessly biased versus start-up, early stage and small caps, as well as the community of securities dealers, attorneys, accountants and IR/PR professionals who work that side of the street. We witnessed this in the recent tacit, and soon to be legitimized, approval of Facebook type transactions (which are really unregistered offerings) and the proliferation of the Second Market's. My hat's-off to their motley crew, but why not let everyone play?

I'm conflicted somewhat because I still admire Marc Andreessen and would hitch hike to the west coast to have lunch with him, even though he is shilling for his VC buddies. Marc believes that only Silicon Valley can identify, structure and price all the "legitimate" early stage opportunities and then keep them from the public markets until his buddies have gorged themselves with enough shares so that the "public" will be lucky to participate at the top while insiders bail out (Loser's Weepers, Finders, Keepers").

Despite my rabble rousing I concur that we need a 'Regulated Wall Street' and all the baby-sitting that it requires for Wall Street denizens, but in a reconstituted way, so that Main Street is represented. That virtual freeway needs lanes dedicated to companies that need to access public markets in order to achieve a size and scope that produces jobs, wealth, and well-being. The names, faces, industries and technologies will change, but the resulting prosperity is what we must strive for. That requires an SEC which embraces, appreciates, and encourages the engine that delivered those economic green shoots, along with politicians that need to stop flogging our public markets. I doubt they will cease being "self-serving", but our financial regulation should be righted with an overhaul, one that mandates both a structural change and an attitude that addresses the bias of a one-size fits all mentality to the exclusion of on-deck participants.

The solution is self-evident. If you have "green" and can be "served" you shouldn't be considered "second-class". If your check clears you've made the squad. And just because you heard about the opportunity via the airways as opposed to being on a call list, you shouldn't be barred from the party. Why not an SEC that recognizes a two-tiered investor platform? I'm not sure where the cut-off point is, and I imagine that mine is further down a mean point than what others might envision, but my sense is that we liberate all companies that have a market value of under $100 million (a separate discussion in any event), leaving the major leaguers with what's already in place.

For the emancipated, and their legions that I trust will follow, the SEC will remain the cop on the beat; one that not only upholds law and order, but hopefully fully appreciates that our democratic/capitalistic system helped create an economy for the benefit of the many. What is vital to its continuance, i.e., ensuring a better life for the millennials that will be paying a great price for our previous transgressions, is that the SEC needs to become more of an "enabler". They need a mental and psychological restart so that their "us versus them", water torture mind set is a thing of the past. If over-regulation is the bane of economic progress than anything that smacks of regulatory malpractice, i.e., forgetting how we got here in the first place, must not be condoned. There needs to be a love fest between both the representatives of the issuer (the guy looking for $) and the toll keepers (regulators) so that commerce can flow through the veins of our business community at speeds the preponderance of our population deserves.

I'm also waiting for the day when a food stamp recipient looks at the guy getting out of the limo and says, "Hi Brother", and truly means it, and a recognition of the unfortunate decline in the ability to access the markets for capital formation through the traditional IPO process. The wave of reverse mergers, SPACS, etc., was a result of crushing the broker/dealer network that could not live with the 1/8's and 1/4's that enriched their larger brethren. We need to go back to a system that rewards those who do the work and need the equivalent of a living wage. It makes perfect sense to pay 6% for a $100m underwriting, but an early stage $10M IPO needs double that to cover the necessities. And by the way, the $10M raise might just as easily create more jobs than its bigger brother.

The challenge to survive and endure by the innovators who work within the system has created new hybrids over the years; the reverse merger, the convertible "bridge", the PIPE, the SPAC, and a regrouping and realignment of past competitors. Technology generally triumphs, and the bulletin and message boards, along with a multitude of day traders, have carved out additional market space that cannot be controlled by the wire houses, investment and traditional banks and a cadre of institutional investors.

This is evidenced by the proliferation of internet "platforms" that are essentially (at least for the near-term) information disseminators that have unlocked doors, hitherto impenetrable, by exploiting the miraculous reach of the internet. Podcasts have become the poor man's answer to the barrier of entry enjoyed by the advertising bridge keepers. They broadcast throughout the globe and reach audiences hitherto unimaginable for the early stage set. While we have to be mindful of the Wolves of Wall Street, a lot of "good intentions" are the breeding grounds for subversive activity. How does one defend the victimization of the so called "99%" by their state governments who forced them to slack their thirst for venturesome investment, by encouraging them to "bet against the House," by giving the no alternative but a tax driven substitute- Keno, Lottery, Scratch tickets, and 'regulated' Casino's, only a stone's throw away from public transportation. On second thought, if history is a precursor to tomorrow's reality, our politicians will keep adding insult to injury while they make sure that they can continue to trade on inside information. What more can I say after Disney married Cinderella to Draft Kings.

Here's to a future where everyone has a fair and reasonable chance to succeed if they work at it and play by the rules. And here's to a rejuvenated two-tiered market system that recognizes the different weight classes and doesn't penalize the little guy because he isn't part of the establishment.

As for me, I don't want to "exit" from the grandstands but from the playing field. "Bury my Heart at Wounded Knee?", No Way! Mail my ashes to every innovation lab you possibly can, with instructions to use as fertilizer on as many new projects as possible. In fact, I'm an entrepreneur's hermaphrodite, having been sexually aroused by their species since I fashioned the first goalies' face mask, and paid $100 to the Boston Bruins' goalie to call it The Harry Lumley Face Saver.

Taking a knee for the moment, another title for my memoir could have been "The Pros and Cons of Co-habiting with Entrepreneurs". That said, as a Johnny Walker Black warms my innards I will wax poetic and remind my reader that I am protected by the phrase "Best Efforts" in what has become a "Show Me the Money" world. What it also means is that my entrepreneur, MY Guy, the exec leading the charge, couldn't attract a legitimate VC; a fact that should be more than enough reason to have you put this book down and having me going back to the drawing board. For better or worse, I've been infected by the people I've made my business to bed, and there's no antidote. Consider the following: the entrepreneur has been defined and portrayed in so many different guises it makes the three blind men who described the elephant omnipotent.

So, what are some of the pros and cons of letting entrepreneurs into your life? The cons can be devastating so a good sense of humor, as you take the verbal abuse from invective investors is de rigueur. The result is a complete overhaul of your original business plan, perhaps several times, leading to investor withdrawal and sleepless nights. But if you want to stay the course and leave a legacy beyond the grandchildren, you need to figure out a way to live with failure, establish and embrace new opportunities, and not abandon the enormous promise and potential of ideas being bandied about at your local Starbucks.

This means bedding members of a mixed tribe that inflict pain in ways that defy the imagination. I've lived with this reality for years, supported their dreams and fancies and rooted them on. I continually make excuses for them, especially to their 'partners' and I've had to send more than my share of Western Union money orders to impoverished entrepreneurs who are behind on their payrolls and their mortgage and car payments.

I've got to admit that I'm still not certain what an entrepreneur is, but I can tell you one thing, 100% of those I work with are more emotional and dedicated than any group that one could imagine. They'll both please and disappoint you, often at the same time, and many of them should be "committed", and not left to their own devices.

Who or what is an Entrepreneur? Call my cell @ 781 389-9703 if you have an answer for me. The following attempts to define and describe the species recognize some piece of the whole, at least I think they're worthy of your attention. Except for my plagiarizing Branson, Hoffman, Zell, and Bussgang (I liked what they said). The rest of the definitions come from my friends, many of whom are also my co-conspirators.

"An Entrepreneur is many things: a job creator, a game-changer, a business leader, an innovator, a disrupter. Most importantly, that entrepreneur is you, if you want to be one badly enough." Sir Richard Branson

"An entrepreneur is someone who will jump off a cliff and assemble an airplane on the way down." Reid Hoffman

"Entrepreneurship is living a few years of your life like most people won't, so you can spend the rest of your life like most people can't." (???)

"Indifference to rejection is a fundamental part of being an entrepreneur." Sam Zell ("Am I Being Too Subtle?")

"Someone with vision beyond the horizon; follows his own compass." Chris Jennings

"An entrepreneur is someone who can identify an unmet need and then, often at peril to himself, puts his heart and soul into meeting that need, generally in a manner not thought of by others." Janice DiPietro, Exceptional Leaders International

"An entrepreneur is someone who looks into the depths of hell and tries to find a path out." John Masiz, BioPhysics Labs

The next 3 are from Dan Ross-(He's someone you want to listen to)

1."A new entrepreneur asks the world "why not?" An experienced entrepreneur knows not "why not", and figures out how to do it anyway."
2."Given the odds of success, if the definition of insanity is repeating what has not worked in the past, are not most entrepreneurs insane?"
3."Entrepreneurs are like alchemists, mixing a spray of passion, a dash of vision, and a pinch of execution to create gold."

"Someone who sees opportunity where other people see risk." Atty. Jan Schlichtmann

"Entrepreneurs make intriguing visionaries- storytellers who carve out a segment of the future and supremely focus to refine a concept through unrelenting effort. Not all visionaries share this fire in the belly, but entrepreneurs do, as passion becomes the requirement for success." Aaron Neiderhelman

"Eternal and many times irrational optimist, whose passion creates boundless energy in order to overcome all the traditional hurdles." Vince Molinari

"Entrepreneurs are the fathers and mothers of invention. Need is the catalyst behind their creation and their motivation, and although inspired by need, it is closely associated with greed." Shelly Kraft

"Short answer: 1. Gambler 2. Adrenalin junkie. A longer answer takes two hours and a scotch." Mark Friedman

"Entrepreneurs do what they like, instead of trying to like what they do." Jim Ramella, CitiCorp

"He's a visionary who sees new opportunities and attempts to profit from them."   Gregory Piatetsky-Shapiro

"An entrepreneur never gives up on a dream or idea and will pursue to fulfillment no matter obstacles and naysayers-and in spite of how battered his shoes look!" Nick Menonna,

"One who sees a need in the marketplace and determines what's necessary to satisfy it, hopefully at a profit." George Schussel

"An entrepreneur is someone who is inspired by solving problems rather than a paycheck. Entrepreneur's think of what will happen if their ideas succeed rather than if they fail." Bill Power, CitiCorp

"The greatest thrill in life is to win. The second greatest thrill is to lose. Tragedy is to never have played the game." Vince Farrell

"An endangered species, migrating off-shore due to climate change, overheated regulation in a capital formation desert." Roland Savage

"Like the Apollo 13th astronauts, the entrepreneur knows that despite being low on life support and operational systems, his best option is still to press forward in hopes of being propelled around the moon. He knows that if anyone is capable of success and survival in this suicide mission, it's he and his crew." Jesse Lopez

"Passion is definitely a key ingredient. As Emerson said, "Nothing great is achieved without enthusiasm." Harry McCoy

"A borderline psychotic, who through a combination of luck, perseverance, contacts, and maxing out his personal credit, turns his dreams into reality." Rock Griffin

"An entrepreneur is an incurable optimist who refuses to accept defeat." Dave Conway

"It's the trapped mouse facing the big bad cat that says, 'The hell with it, I'll go for his balls". Joe Valente

"Entrepreneurs are the new heroes as they make things happen, in spite of government interference." Rick Brutti

"An entrepreneur is someone with an idea, who knows a good banker and is willing to work 100 hours a week indefinitely." Jane O'Shaughnessy

"HE spoke the world into existence. There is a true entrepreneur!" Sergio Garcia

"A 19th century philosopher spoke of "Creative Destruction", which is a change in activity whenever a new product or process enters the marketplace. An entrepreneur seeks to fundamentally refine it or reshape it to its highest performance level." Ralph Edelstein

"An entrepreneur is 20 percent dreamer and 90 percent doer; a master at getting people to do it his way and has great patience but wants it now." Steve Swartz

"Nothing in the world can take the place of persistence. Talent will not; nothing is more common than unsuccessful men with talent. Genius will not; unrewarded genius is almost a proverb. Education will not; the world is full of educated derelicts. Persistence and determination alone are omnipotent." Atty. Bill Gildea (He stole this from Calvin Coolidge)

"Entrepreneurs do not retire to Florida before the job is done!" Elliot Klugman

"Entrepreneurs believe that sleep is over-rated." John Morelli

"An insane masochist who sees no other choice!" David Batsford

"An entrepreneur creates businesses and opportunities for the sake of achievement and personal satisfaction." Wayne Webster

"An entrepreneur is a promoter with substance, a delicate mixture of legality, morality, ethics, aggression and failure." Richard Patterson

"Safety nets are less of a net and more of a spider's web." Ron Davis (While teaching, Ron's class adopted the rhino as the symbol for entrepreneurialism because (a) they have thick-skin and (b) can only move forward)

"Testicular fortitude is a key trait." Mike Magliochetti

"They are self-declared dreamers. They think about big ideas and then make them happen. When the idea becomes reality, they don't fully appreciate its success and understand that their role is over." David Platt

"Entrepreneurs are an enigma. They embrace it by default; at once repulsed by bosses, restrictive boundaries and limitations from third parties. They set their own goals and limitations, and although not necessarily by self-design, are unavoidably leaders. They are usually less than satisfied with subordinates with inferior execution skills, and are only close to being satisfied when one of their subordinates demonstrates similar skills, which usually result in them having to watch their own backs. They live a life of feast or famine." Woody" Woodworth

"An entrepreneur is someone who can take threads of gold from others' ideas, recombine them with a spark of something extra, overlay with creativity and passion, and make something to which others will say, "Why didn't I think of that?" Jo Broderick

"A driver who executes what is right, or needed, despite obstacles, resistance, or ensuing defeat." Tom Fleury

"An entrepreneur is someone who has an innate motivation to transform his or her business vision into reality irrespective of available resources and conventional wisdom. A successful entrepreneur inspires other people to participate in this transformation as employees, investors, advisors and advocates, and through these efforts, attracts a growing number of loyal customers." Rusty Williams

"The entrepreneur is a driven personality that will 'make it happen' despite the odds of success that may not be in his/her favor. 'Making it happen' is the drive to change that part of the world over which the entrepreneur's abilities, passion, and vision can proactively influence the outcome. The entrepreneur accepts profit as the reward for challenging the status quo and the world." Tim Cyr

"Someone who burns with passion for a purpose that finds no home in ridged structures that he/she did not co-create, who embraces being regarded as "unreasonable", or a "dreamer", knowing that greatness occurs at the edge of the cliff and that being alive means being unsafe." Bridget Cooper

"There is something innate about being an entrepreneur; an internal compass that sometimes unknowingly, steers a person away from the beaten path. They may hone our skills in corporate hallways for a while, but eventually they become thoroughly unemployable. They want to set own direction, believe in their own journey, make their own decisions, establish their own norms and values, grow deaf at the naysayers, embrace creativity, risk taking and decisiveness, and grow increasingly intolerant of moderation and the inept bystanders that espouse it's alleged virtue. They make no excuses, take no prisoners and rarely sit back to admire their work, because they instinctively know that business is a contact sport!" Thom Stimpel

CHAPTER 7

The following are some of my Letter's to the Editor and letters to my "Friends". Hopefully this will not alert the authorities to monitor my day to day activities more closely. I'm also counting on my handicap parking sign, cane and walker to play the sympathy card. Since this will only get me so far, I ask that you send contributions to any defense or assistance program established in the future on my behalf.

"I believe that what defines us is the way we treat others. It should be with respect and kindness. If not given in return, take it from where it comes and continue to forge ahead, making new relationships and taking care of your responsibilities."

"Our 'Tax-payer Funded Addiction' (NYT's 11/11/17) was fully exposed in depth in Sam Quinones' "Dream Land", the sordid history of opioid addiction in the U.S, and those who profited from its use. Unfortunately, Mr. Quinones' conclusion that there is no "Holy Grail", no chance for a non-addictive substitute for opioids, is incorrect and tragic. His message has had a negative impact on those politicians and advisors controlling the purse strings of the $3B set aside by President's Obama and Trump. – and for those who want to do something about debilitating pain and its consequences, ask your doctor about a recently filed a provisional patent covering the delivery of ibuprofen and gabapentin simultaneously; the results of which could solve the addiction problem for the largest patient population affected."

"The NYTimes should be applauded for its coverage of the "Opioid Epidemic"; two of many examples being Nicholas Kristof's "How to Win the War on Drugs" (9/24/17), which reported on the way that Portugal treats addiction, i.e., "as a medical problem not a criminal justice issue"; and in "Breaking Opioid Addiction", (10/1/17), which suggested a variety of ways to save addict's lives, as well as the need to inform those in danger.

This is admirable reporting and certainly a far cry from other very important issues of today which 'finger point' rather than educate. However, it does not address, nor is it an answer that helps the largest segment of our addicted population, that of which is composed of the injured and wounded, as well as the older working and retired men and women who have pain so severe, pervasive and persistent, that only opioids can help them. These are not the people who populate our prisons, nor overdose for pleasure. They nevertheless endure many of the same consequences as those who became addicted for other reasons.

President's Obama and Trump, and almost everyone who has expressed deep concern re opioid addiction have pledged to fight this scourge, made it #1 on their agenda, set aside Billions to invest in helping to eradicate it, but have not followed through with grants that truly address the issue.

As an example, Massachusetts , in spite of the endorsement of Republican Governor Charley Baker, Democratic minority leader Bruce Tarr, and support from UMass Medical School, a Massachusetts based pharma which has recently filed a patent for a non-addictive alternative to opioids, has had to look to dubious investors who ask the same question- 'If it's so good, why hasn't a single dime been spent from Federal funds?'

I'm sending you this letter in hopes that you call attention to our need to identify private citizens and/or institutions that would contact us and do the due diligence that those entrusted to do it, have not."

"The Market Is Shrinking, and That's a Problem" (Jeff Sommer-Strategies-NYT's 8/5/18) was a result of overzealous regulators co-habiting with investment bankers, brokerage firms and VC's. This tilted the playing field so that entrepreneurs and their supporters have become beholden to predators, having lost access to our so-called "Free Market". This need not at a time when the internet has given a voice to anyone who can use this platform to sell their vision to potential early stage investors who do their own research. These potential investors may not be Accredited, but they are Knowledgeable.

Our regulators have also recognized the need to expand the options for companies who want to use the public markets as an alternative to the more restrictive and costly regulations of the past. Working capital via marketable securities is a far better option for entrepreneurs and their early stage Friends and Family supporters versus the costs and restrictive nature of the current sources of equity for entrepreneurs. At the same time, there has been exponential growth in the dissemination of information on all fronts and the populace has become armed with mobile devices, cell phones, lap tops, and has easy access to knowledge (Google, Siri, etc.), as well as the social media platforms (Facebook, Twitter,
etc.).

There's also been a much greater interest in entrepreneurship by institutional investors given the Unicorn phenomena and the returns enjoyed by first movers. Witness to this is their embrace and adoption by HBS, where better than 50% of the second-year class are being taught by venture capitalists, who no longer reference Uber as their poster boy but have found plenty of fodder to replace it. When many of this year's graduating class face the hard reality that 75% of tech start-ups either fail or do not reach profitability within four years of founding, they'll be fodder for their handlers unless they have saner alternatives, i.e., small, best efforts, IPO's offered by a new breed of underwriters who are under the watchful eye of compliance professionals and early-stage investment pros, while being devoid of any stock brokers, thus ensuring much lower expenses and fewer regulatory liabilities."

Ltr. NYT's 7/16- "I took Andrew Ross Sorkin's advice and read Mohamed A. El-Erian's "The Only Game In Town". Brilliantly written but prejudicial in both his examination and explanation of the 'bail-out' and the ensuing Fed handling of the 2008 economic meltdown and stock market crash. Unfortunately for most Americans, the title of Mohamed's book says it all. The architects, Hank Paulson, Ben Bernanke, Bob Rubin, Larry Summers and Tim Geithner (all now gainfully employed or tied to the umbilical cord of the Wall Street Crowd) had other options but opted for a game that only a few could play, which ultimately resulted in a path that a preponderance of our citizenry are now struggling to recover from. Mohamed's "new normal of low growth, rising inequality, political dysfunction and in some cases social tensions – all despite massive policy interventions on the part of central banks", suggests that he still hasn't figured it out: It isn't "despite of", it's "because of" ; what we needed was an enema not a banquet."

Ltr. NYT's 8/13- "Gretchen Morgenson's 'Neglecting to Name Names': Gretchen, why beat a dead horse? Even American Pharoah is retiring. The buyers of these CITI investments have signed off as "Accredited" (sophisticated). If there's a beef to be made, it should come from the CITI shareholders themselves who hadn't a clue what their high-priced leaders had conjured up to bilk their clients, to up their revenues and bonuses. At the least a whistle blower suit should have been instituted. Unfortunately, CITI shareholders have been denied their pound of flesh by a Statute of Limitations that needs updating to account for fraudulent behavior that should toll the when uncovered. At the least, we need to find additional fertile grounds for all of the tort attorneys who are still struggling with non-dischargeable student loans taken out when they too were 'Unsophisticated'

"Up until my 60th reunion at Harvard Business School, I would have argued that the Age of the Unicorn didn't portend a market bubble. After all, valuations established by those supposedly in the know, and representing non-public, relatively early stage technology wonder-kin, didn't, nor should they, represent the valuations in our public markets. They vie with the markets at Sotheby's, not at E-Trad. So what changed my mind? -My beloved B School has embraced the entrepreneur, pivoting from the bastion of corporate America (read- the industrialized world) to sacrificing generations of talented, motivated, educated world beaters, by advocating, with more than religious zeal, the opportunities and excitement of being your own boss today, or a member of a group that bonds itself in a Seal-like take-no-prisoners commercial activity, embraces business celibacy, and succeeds because, 'where there is a will there is a way'.

One would have thought they learned their lesson. Interviews for Goldman and Citi are now held off campus and, God forbid, no one with any standing in the community would mention that they accepted a job in Oshkosh as opposed to Silicon Valley. General Doriot is probably turning in his grave and the banks that gave HBS'ers their student loans better downgrade their quality. But what do I know? When I touched on the risks associated with the assumptions in our simulated classes, I was shut-out of any discussion. Our current professors don't give much credence to feet on the ground for a reasonable period of time; they keep muttering Face Book, Uber. My point is that I wish that institutions of higher learning would stop using the entrepreneurial theme as a poster boy to extol their own interests. They have no idea of the pain they will be inflicting on many of the students they are entrusted to educate and should be cited for sending graduates into a world that will quickly eat them up. I'm sure if you took a poll of the so-called business school educators you'd find a vast difference in how they each defined the species they are encouraging, nay promoting to conquer all. By creating a category of "in business" people that have a special aura unto themselves, exclusive hierarchy in the pantheon pursuing the almighty dollar- a deity of specificity- the pain and suffering will be more intensive and pervasive than is necessary. True entrepreneurs are not made; they come out of a mold that defies reproduction."

"Bubble in the market? – not in securities, but for the better than 55% of current HBS students who will most likely be looking for jobs five to seven years out, and find that their classmates are drinking Champaign while they're looking for change to buy another Bud."

"There's a huge cost to "compromise", and its undertaking will strain a lot of relationships, but the alternatives are not options worth considering. As we listen to the candidates for 2016 let's get behind someone who can bridge our great divide and get us back on the road to an economic recovery that rewards those willing to pick up a shovel or its equivalent, rather than stand around with a sign and a bull horn. If we don't engage in meaningful dialogue and respect those who are in an opposite camp, all sides will suffer but for the very few who will always be above the fray. More importantly, the opportunity to move this great democracy forward will elude us for still another incumbency. Please keep this in mind as you listen to the candidates. Your vote and support is perhaps more important to your future and that of your family than at any previous time."

"What fate is awaiting the Jockeys that were led to believe that they could ride Unicorns into the sunset. While those on the west coast will think I'm off my rocker, I compare many of these wunderkind to the Ponzi's, and Madoff's of the past. Not that this new breed are candidates for our corrections system; more likely they've drunk the cool-aid themselves and are overcome with the rapture of the maddening crowd. What's amazing to me is the adoption of the belief in many prestigious business schools that to the extent they can enlist the brightest of the bright to embark on the procreation of this beast, even though its life-cycle and the unique window that spawned it, is doomed it to self-implosion. These institutions base their insistence on what they believe is self-evident- the entrepreneur is the new superman and can overcome anything with help from their faculty. I pray for these kids. It's one thing to be saddled with college debts, it's another to keep from advancing in the business arena while being guini pigs for their instructors who fashion themselves as the 'masters of the universe'. "

"Maybe there are some who can live alone, buttressed by their own thoughts and withdrawn from the joys of human contact. I cannot. Living a good life has many meanings but underneath it all is mutual respect. If it's not there then there is really no relationship of substance/meaning. In the long run we need to be proud of the way we have conducted ourselves in any relationship. We are all taking the same voyage the remains of which will be the fond memories, the feeling of companionship, brotherhood, loyalty and love that will strengthen us in many ways."

"Greed and corruption are pervasive and well camouflaged. Ditto for bull-shit artists and con men. Don't be sucked into the maelstrom. Due Diligence is not an option; and don't count on Face Book, Google and Linked-In be the totality of your homework. Make the calls and check out the neighborhood. There's no reason that you have to support their life style."

"Two recent headlines, "Elizabeth Warren Joins Call To Tighten Investment Broker Rules" and "Obama Proposes New Standard On Retirement Advice", creates more unnecessary regulation and red tape without proffering a solution. If in fact Warren and Obama want to protect, reward, and insure those that choose to invest in a sound, riskless and rewarding way for their retirement, should simply set up a government fund where those investors can send money at no cost, and let our government use these funds in any way, guarantee that those funds are secure, accrue and compound interest at a rate equal to the ongoing treasury rate plus the Feds inflation rate, as well as a combination of the S&P and Dow Jones averages."

"Our treasury mavens insist that "retirement assets merit special protection", the inference being that somehow the current free market system is not appropriate for investment of these funds, so why not index returns on treasuries to the rate our Triple A corporations pay. On second thought, why not let anyone invest in the same retirement funds that our Congressmen and Senators have? What is it by the way?"

"It's becoming fashionable for entrepreneurs to go into rapture when discussing their failures, or so reports the New York Times. Actually, the "telling" is more like a broadcasting of a stellar event in that the ongoing use of social networks to disseminate one's fall, and all that it implies, is designed to hail the fallen hero, and present him (or her) with a Purple Heart, as if they defended the Alamo and were awarded for their stupidity in not leaving the building when they had a chance the night before. And there are a lot of medals to go around, especially when you consider that 40% of all startups fail before their first anniversary, 80% never achieve profitability, and liquidity for investors is enjoyed by only a few.

But don't let the facts get in the way of stopping you from making money by going at risk. There's a simple way to up your long odds for success; make sure you are not investing in early stage companies that haven't a plan to be public in or within the next 18 months, or are not receptive to public ownership, since they think they can get angel or VC investors to provide the capital to get to break-even (and even more). Whether it's an IPO, reverse-merger into a public company, or For Sale sign, its thumbs down if otherwise. That, of course, is not a guarantee of an investor making money in or within his lifetime, but it is the path that gives you and your fellow investors a fighting chance. It also suggests that if you want to play the game of 10 baggers, you are better off trolling through the legions of would be Steve Jobs that get interviewed and examined by Shelly and his crew, than by getting the House odds and having no alternative but to sit, and sit, and sit. Give me liquidity or give me death."

"I wish that most of our business schools would stop using the entrepreneurial theme as a poster boy to extol their own interests. They either have no idea of the pain they are inflicting on the future of many of the students they are supposedly educating, or they should be cited for sending graduates into a world that will quickly eat them up. I'm sure if you took a poll of the so-called business school educators you'd find a vast difference in how they each defined the species they are encouraging, nay extolling, to 'innovate' as a major and forget about the on the job training they still need to pursue to hone business acumen and specificity and become much more grounded and elite as business pro's. Where will these educators be when their alumni come back for references so they can get a real job? "

"Entrepreneurs are not made; they come out of a mold that defies reproduction. If the urge takes over by the time they get into graduate school chances are they're having bad dreams and should be sent to rehab and the suburbs, not Cambridge."

"Happiness is a result of managing expectations and adapting to changing circumstances. You do not have to accept the status quo, but you have to be realistic in assessing your own capabilities and appreciating the needs of those whose lives you affect and, in the alternative, those who affect yours."

"There is nothing wrong with setting goals and standards that prove challenging, but there will most likely be setbacks that you need to think of as temporary side roads which simply delay your ultimate objective. You need to be able to smile at the end of the day and rack up everything to experience. Tomorrow is what it is all about."

"As both a leader and member of a team, respect other's opinions, but be not afraid to challenge their ideas and suggestions. Vet them thoroughly. At the end of the day you're the one that's responsible for the any decisions made; and you have to be prepared to live with the consequences."

"It isn't always about being right, it's about winning at the end of the day. Winning is being able to do the things that you want to do. And it's not only about money. We all have different "tastes" (personal) and different "objectives". Think of the following, as the days tick by, what kind of a life do you want to look back on? What legacy do you want to leave?"

"If Christ, Abraham and Mohammed re-examined their rhetoric they would most likely concede that some of their teachings/beliefs might need some updating. Let's face it, I doubt that anyone who has anything to say with respect to what others should do- how they should conduct themselves, is walking a fault line that probably needs some shoring up. I can't fault them completely (they have an agenda and God bless them for their entrepreneurial endeavors); but if they don't know the difference between what is factual/believable, and what might be referred as voodoo, they're really dangerous. Unfortunately, others infected with this proclivity are reporters, pundits and politicians."

"Geithner's bail-out created unintended consequences of such monumental proportion that they far outweigh any supposed benefits. How do you measure the cost associated with the explosion of the cry for entitlement; Can you blame the 99% for demanding "If them, why not me?" Where is it written? Is it in the Old/New Testament, the Koran, the Constitution or perhaps the Pledge of Allegiance? Is it simply an Old Wife's Tale? And why is it taking the time, energy, and cost that otherwise could be put to better use in seeking a way out of this economic mess?"

"What I'm looking for is the law that says that we have to bail out anyone. I keep hearing that we should be thankful for those geniuses that gave us TARP. That was relatively easy to sell using the opioids at the time, but now that that demagogy is behind us I'm hoping clearer minds will see the forest from the trees. Perhaps not seeing that we now are considering that we might have to bail out mutual funds that might not be able to give back investors what they put up? That we- the working stiffs - have to make good if someone gets back less than dollar for dollar? Give us a brake (as in 'Break the Buck'). Simple fix; make those funds that are in that business make the print larger when talking about risks so there's no cry-babying later. Instead of insulting our intelligence, let's do something like creating one new job before adding to ballooning government funded staffs whose only justification is their need to further justify their existence by placing additional red-tape on overburdened and beleaguered businesses."

"I'm still amazed, still in love with the thought, fascinated by it, that you can take an idea, an activity, a virtual, pre-revenue, early stage entrepreneurial activity, raise money from investors (individuals and institutional), go to the public markets, and even after you've changed direction, focus, and your team, have an opportunity to create something of commercial value for employees, customers, investors and whoever the multiplier affect applies to. Why is it that our politicians and regulators don't understand and appreciate the beauty, simplicity and value that this represents? Forget about "Rise Above"; our new mantra should be "Embrace!"

"It's not that long ago that we were treated to a parade of gravitas from the savants housed on the banks of the Charles. They were tending to the self-inflicted wounds of their investment banking buddies by convincing both our regulators and legislators that we should pick up the tab for a Wall Street party we weren't invited to. Having sold us out, its four years later and any excuse or pretense that it was the only way out flies in the face of the failure to get an affirmative answer to the basic question – "Are we truly better off today and are we still hopeful about our future?"

"Behind and beyond the rhetoric, the next fight, debate, decision of our Pols revolves around who should get what, where it should come from, and who should pay for it. We have become a nation of "takers", wasting the assets of what used to be the ballast of the good old U.S. of A."

"Next time someone who works for the government and never had to meet a payroll or punch a time clock makes you a promise (essentially tells you that he will "put it in" without any consequence and if it doesn't work out will pay for child support), pee on his foot and tell him it's raining. That's what I call tit for tat."

"A real-time all out search by MIT Data Miners was conducted for the European Union and the United States to use sentiment analysis to pick out the best place for each to hold an economic summit. As a result, the next meeting of the Leaders of the so called Free World will be held in Lourdes, with the US leadership having a choice of either Fantasy Island or Disney World."

"My votes for sale. I'm ready to give it to the first candidate that declares war on unemployment. If Obama doesn't do it before the election, Mitt should pledge to do it within the first 30 days if he is elected. I don't care if Mitt didn't pay taxes or our Pres cannot find his birth certificate".

"We've got millions of casualties and everyone is looking the other way. We should take no prisoners. Why are we talking about everything else? I don't care about the "fiscal cliff" nor does our youth, soldiers coming home, or the over 50's who have been put out to pasture by anyone who would work for less, especially those that I have to speak to before getting someone at home that will handle my complaint."

"Shovel ready? Hell, there isn't anyone with half a brain that wouldn't know where to spend money to get our engine cranked up. We're at war and are playing pussy. WTF!"

"What makes everyone think that things are always tougher in their world? Let's stop making excuses for mediocrity. Just step to the plate and "execute". If that's not good enough, dust yourself off (the youngsters call it "pivoting"; earlier generations said it was "repositioning"; we called it "changing direction"). It's simply admitting a mistake and using your remaining capital till it, or you, are exhausted."

"As for thinking differently; sounds good when you hear or read it but its fiction. It reminds me of "Do more with less"; less than what? "Think differently about leadership"? You either pick up the baton or you get in line and don't blame others."

"The stage is finally set and the electorate will have a very easy choice to make- as in- Which came first, the chicken or the egg? As if it really matters. This question was inherent in the declaration by President Obama that it was our government- all of its branches, regulatory bodies, etc. not our free enterprise system- entrepreneurs, robber barons, capitalists, business leaders, etc. who were responsible (should get the credit) for what we lovingly call "The Good Old USofA". He's put forth his credo with the presumption that his opponent represents the other side. I guess this also means that, depending on the victor, we will get more of the same. Either way, I certainly hope not. Depending upon how you feel, you can either vote for the chicken or for the egg."

"Most of us come into this world with love, and that's about it. Expectations come over time and are dictated by those who we associate with, are surrounded by, or upon whom we can credit or place blame. It is what it is. So where does this "entitlement" thing come from?"

"Let's face it kids (all of us), mom and dad probably loved you and gave you a lot of support- material and other wise- and if it wasn't there for you (perceived or otherwise) there were very few who really cared. What's the point? Entitlement is a fiction. The sooner you realize it the better your life can be. So either plan for it (education, work ethic, etc.) or get used to standing in line with a tin cup waiting for our politicians to send you some checks in exchange for your vote. By the way, what will that vote be?"

"A ruling in a federal court said that the SEC has to be "fair and even-handed"; what a laugh? It is more than being "fair"; that's only the first step on the long road back to our "Made in America" system. It meant jobs and a standard of living for anyone who was willing to work and take risks. It is almost unimaginable to me that our system is now so disemboweled by regulators that there is a more than even chance that entrepreneurs, capitalists and investors can be summarily dismissed from participating in what we used to believe was a democracy that functioned under the rule of law. Let's take back our country! "

"I'm all for regulation; it's an essential part of a democratic, capitalistic society. The question is simply, on a case by case basis, does it serve its purpose or does it inhibit the future growth and prosperity that it was intended to protect and foster? Furthermore, in its implementation, are our regulators, however diligent and devoted they may be, even-handed in their pursuit of possible offenders, or are they misguided and arbitrary in exercising their power, particularly in their treatment of those in the commercial activities that they are empowered to oversee? My next comments are not meant to lessen authority or to protect anyone crossing what sometimes is almost the faintest of lines. It's to bring a rationale to a system that has not protected the interests of everyone in the game, and has produced consequences that we are paying too high a price to let go unchanged."

"There is no one "fix", no panacea, no Holy Grail. And for that reason we have to agree on "priorities" and forget for the moment about trade-offs and political posturing (perhaps too much to expect). My vote is for job creation in the private sector, a topic always espoused but very rarely addressed, except for pet political projects and grandstanding government investments that no sane, intelligent investor would go at risk for."

"One obvious way is through the repatriation of the overseas profits that many of our major corporations are keeping offshore. There's no doubt that, either through the dividends they may produce to U.S. shareholders (which are then taxed, banked, invested or spent), or the use in expanding employment and/or buying goods and services here, and paying some minimum tax, this 'stroke of the pen' is a "no-brainer".

"My recommendation goes to another job creator- investment in start-up or early stage companies which investors, not politicians or government agencies, deem worthy of risk. For a variety of reasons, not the least of which is the burdensome costs associated with their financing, these companies have been excluded from our capital markets because the platforms and support systems that once offered them access to the public markets have been either neutered or destroyed by a system that embraced size and exclusivity and priced everyone else out of the marketplace."

"Am I wrong? Wasn't it all supposed to be about Jobs? If so, we don't have to debate the issue. $800B was spent (equivalent to $10,000 for every homeowner- talk about stimulus and shovel ready construction jobs; or trips to the market, the mall, etc.) and even in high school eco classes we were aware that this equated to a "multiplier effect". However, we did get a predictable stock market lift (very high marks for that), and an eventual fairly significant increase in real estate valuations, all of which were paid for by those people who believed that saving was a virtue, as well as paying your bills in a timely fashion.

So how about tackling what has already been agreed to is the most important thing we can do for our citizens and do it in a way that recognizes/ acknowledges that the government cannot, but the private sector can, put money to work in job creation where the chances for commercial success are far more apt to take place? Let's also add another extremely important ingredient. When "We the People" go at risk, someone else has to also suffer if we have to take a loss.

Simple formula to jump-start our economy. Create QE-4 to match, dollar for dollar, any equity investment made by new investors. Our "investment" is conditioned on the following: Companies/projects that we underwrite need to be valued at less than $100m so that we are not continuously supporting the largest donors to both parties. They also need to create one new job for every $50,000 we lend to the project. Principals of the borrower are limited in both salary and equity conversion until 50% of our money is repaid. To further incentivize investors (those truly at risk) they get capital gains tax treatment at the lessor of 20% or their lower marginal rate. More importantly, there is a claw-back. If the number of new jobs does not equate within a six month window to the amount we as taxpayers go at risk for, that portion attributable to a new hire, becomes due and payable to us in/within a six month period.

This program will require a new team to organize, supervise and oversee but we do have agencies that can be reconfigured to assume and meet the task. We know that there will be losses, especially early in the process, but even by making loans far below what we are doing now, this will be a "home-run". My assumption is that 25% of participating businesses will close with an outright loss to us within 3 years (but will have gainfully employed 250,000 workers during that period), that 50% of participating businesses will continue with hires during the five years and then begin to repay over the next 5 years, and that 25% of participating businesses will be able to start repayment at the end of 5 years. All this is debatable of course, but it seems more reasonable in that it will address what is most needed as opposed to the non-performing fantasy game now on display."

"AM KNEE ZURE is that point in time when the entrepreneur has forgotten the implied value of his pro-forma and his investors have lost their tolerance for risk. This phenomenon occurs after the 3rd year of the investment; the disease is usually rampant after the 5th. Cure: None, although a ten-bagger from another long shot and the offset for some tax avoidance greatly diminishes the pain. Antidote: A Rights Offering. Gets rid of the faint of heart and rearrange the deck chairs. Result: For the prior investors who cannot pony up again at a greatly reduced valuation, pain; for those who know a good deal when they see one, the skies the limit; and for the entrepreneur/jockey who is allowed another run for the roses, a much-needed transfusion."

"A preponderance of great innovative ideas never see the light of day because they fall far short of meeting today's marketplace demands. Clayton Chrestenson and some of his HBS buddies would have those managers responsible for growing their operations think as innovators/disrupters and not as marketers that simply reposition If one could invest at the point where concept was taken through to reality, investors would have discovered the Holy Grail. Maybe that's why the expression "Keep your powder dry" has so much more meaning to veterans as opposed to rookies?"

"The 'Jobs Bill' referred to in "Boston's Innovation Economy" is widely regarded as Crowd Funding, and doesn't, as the editorial points out, "require new ways of thinking about investment". Investing is not charity nor is it done primarily for the greater good, nor should it be. The intent of the bill is to make it easier, less expensive, and essentially more viable for start-up, early-stage companies to access all potential investors, not just those that are necessarily "sophisticated" (as in having a high net worth or high current income), and without the excessive costs associated with the process, as is now the case.

That doesn't mean that investors should be sucker-punched any more (or less) than under the present rules of the road. If our regulators will truly lift the present handcuffs to frustrated entrepreneurial activity, we still deserve the kind of information that will allow informed decision making. The key is in the type of disclosure that we all need, i.e., who the officers/directors are (the ones that will control the money raised), how real the market opportunity is, a business plan that gives one a chance to pass judgement, and the professionals (accts/attys/consultants) that have lent their name to the dream."

"Letters@NYTimes.com: Gretchen Morgenson's "At Big Banks, A Lesson Not Learned", leaves out the perpetrators, KKR and Bain Capital; CITI and their ilk were simply their hired guns who knew, if caught, could bail themselves out with investor's money and move on the next high jacking. Elizabeth Warren can add FINRA to her list and make sure that the 20% in 2 and 20 is income, not capital gains."

"Let's admit to petty larceny. In today's Boston Globe they gave high-five's to The Massachusetts Gaming Commission because we took in close to $20M from our citizens in this week's lottery pools. Imagine the better results for everyone if this money was used to purchase food, clothing and shelter."

"The following is not meant to lessen authority or to protect anyone crossing what oftentimes is an imperceptible line. It's to bring a rationale to a system that has failed to protect the interests of all the players and has produced consequences that we are paying too high a price to let go unchallenged:- One size doesn't fit all; Sugar Ray never got into the ring with Ali. In order for the U.S. to have a strong, vibrant, effective market for early stage and emerging small companies, it has to have a brokerage community that can cater to the financial needs of those companies and a clientele that understands the risks and rewards associated with those investments and wants to participate in that market no matter what others might think (I don't see any police at the entrance of casino's or having to show my net worth statement when I buy a scratch ticket).

Let's have a two, or even three tired system, distinguished simply by the size of the companies involved. The regulators (individuals) that oversee these companies should be dedicated to similarly categorized companies. It's no secret (ask any practicing SEC attorney) that there's an "us" versus "them" mentality at the SEC and that there's definitely a bias against smaller, early stage companies, particularly those trying to access the public markets for the first time. The same has been true in the treatment, via fiat or benign neglect, for the smaller brokerage firms over the past two decades. The fact is that they have been squeezed out as a matter of policy, and as a result we are now witnessing the second markets and the altered rules; to wit, the Face Book 'exemption'.

This also means a change in the pricing as it relates to the earlier stage category, both to trading spreads, fractional movements, and investment banking fees. Goldman makes a fortune at 5%; that % doesn't pay for the lights when you are working on a $3-$5M placement. Nor can one pay the legal and accounting fees that are necessitated by an arcane system designed more for the FDA than a market where everyone recognizes that they must assume some modicum of risk."

"I cannot imagine why Bernanke keeps taking a stage coach when he has a blank check account at the Fed. His $80B per month largess, funneled directly to bank vaults, doesn't help solve our "jobs" problem. It's a placebo rather than a cure. You could easily leverage the $80B into $160B without taxpayer risk, and put it in the hands of companies that will hire people or repay it. It would be the catalyst to lever capital from investors who are on the sidelines loath to part with it today but will, when their potential return is fueled by low cost debt and a tax advantaged return, step back into the game."

"It used to be that you were proud to be an American. Sure, there was plenty that had to be changed, but we always seemed to be headed in the right direction and at the end of the day we corrected most of the "errors of our ways". You had a good feeling when you sang the Star Spangled Banner, saluted the flag, or thought about the good old U.S of A. But now, unless the only thing you're interested in is last year's champs, you have to wonder what went wrong and if we can, once again, have faith in our leadership and trust that they will place our well-being ahead of their own special interests."

"I know it's too much to ask, but don't you think that a fair question for every candidate for office is if they would support and/or propose a bill that would give up their special privileges and receive the same benefits with respect to Social Security and Medicare that the vast majority of working people have? Talk about feeling better!"

"I've been looking for a truly descriptive way of epitomizing the relationship that existed between the Wall Street architects of our economic destruction and their Ivy League collaborators (fellow alumni) who saved their asses and forgot about protecting ours; my suggestion: "in flagrante delicto".

"How many seconds would it take you to make up your mind whether you'd vote for an Amendment to the Constitution that would say the following: Congress shall make no law that applies to the citizens of the United States that does not apply to them, nor shall Congress pass laws that pertain to themselves that in the alternative do not pertain to the citizens of the United States."

"My favorite read is Doonesbury, whose sage advice is ever in my mind. Today Zonker suggested we "Trust the Invisible Hand", and later in the day when I took my 'Random Walk Down Wall Street' , I ran into a gaggle of Black Swans while also observing several Barbarians vaulting the NYSE barriers, and felt little fear; I was certain that when the markets opened the my psychotherapist, Becky Quick, would discuss the safety of the swans and the rebuffing of the trespassers. In addition to Warren Buffet, she must talk to Gary Trudeau, Charlie Rose and the world is flat guy before going to bed."

"As you crawl into bed this evening, ask yourself one simple question; what have you done recently to improve the life of someone? And I'll add one caveat; without benefiting yourself."

"I cannot help but think about the change that takes place in our elected officials when they get to Washington; they become infected by the scent of 'green' from the special interest groups. Any lingering thoughts that place their constituents first are soon abandoned. While it's a gradual process, it always seems to follow the same sequence. At first they get a little bit pregnant, then they become "enablers" before morphing into "conspirators". What else? It's on to their next term with a full war chest."

"I was thinking about a way to get someone's attention in D.C.; a way in which one might send an important message (suggestion) to a congressman, senator, presidential advisor, Federal Reserve member, Supreme Court Justice, etc. etc. My best idea was to package any request with a severed horse's head. Seems appropriate and an effective way of making a point.

Who wouldn't believe it? When I called to order a dozen heads as a starter, I was told that there was a three year wait and that payment was fixed at three ounces of gold, prepaid. It appears that The Committee to Scuttle Dodd-Frank, Friends of Drones, hedge fund lobbyists, the likes of Goldman, AIG, the A F of L, and The Ancient and Honorable Libor Enhancers, among others (they're watching me as I write) have cornered the market for Head.

I'm left with one alternative that seems to have a lot of merit. What about a twisted chicken's neck? At today's prices I could send one to everyone in the D.C phonebook. At least there's a practical use for each one; the recipient can turn it in for a tax deduction at the nearest soup kitchen and therefore understand and appreciate the multiplier effect and the true meaning of unintended consequences."

"It is totally appropriate, and probably an ominous sign, that the musical "Annie" is slated for a Broadway comeback; by that time, many more of our citizenry will truly appreciate, and have a personal understanding of what it means to have "A Hard Knock Life". No doubt that Big Daddy Warbucks will be sought after for autographs. His casting call has just gone out and there's a lot of speculation as to who would be best for the role. My bet is Ben Bernanke; he's going to have to keep up his life-support stimulus, or the Sun won't come out tomorrow, you just wait and see!"

"JOBS represent more than the ability to support self and family. They provide the human dignity that responsible, caring citizens need. If we don't provide the platforms that enable/encourage systems that create them, than we as a nation have not met the pre-requisite of good governance and we should seek new leaders to accomplish this. This verity also goes for "safety nets". Many of us, for a multiplicity of reasons, are not "equal"- in the sense of self-supporting- and this has to be a "cost" that all of us bear. If we could acknowledge this, as I believe most of us do, then I have no quarrel (and still whole hardily embrace) the notion of "Self Interest" as somehow working for the benefit of all of us in our democratic, capitalistic society. Survival of the fittest is something we all can live with, even try to emulate, if it is tempered with a dose/sense of humanity."

"It's interesting to see that things haven't changed at Brandeis since my graduation during the last Ice Age. Students can be stirred up easily by faculty, especially in matters where both they and the faculty have very little, if any, personal experience; in this instance compensation for a tenured CEO in a highly competitive and especially difficult environment. Our faculty continue to believe that they are the most important element of the university, and as a group that's true, but, in my humble opinion, not so on an individual basis, no matter their especial brilliance. There are many more outstanding professors than outstanding university CEO's, and their pay, just like professionals in other fields, is established in a very competitive, and to my knowledge, over populated marketplace. To say that Dr. Reinharz was paid/is being paid too much suggests that the Board of Trustees over his rein didn't know what they were doing, i.e., they were oblivious to competitive market conditions, and/or that the faculty members were underpaid.

Let's agree that the primary job of a university president is to raise money and be the face of the university. On this score, Brandeis got more than they bargained for (Hats off to them). In a very tough and competitive fiscal environment, the growth of the university, in all aspects of the campus experience, was extraordinary given the circumstances. That was not a result of the student body, the faculty, or the alumni, but of the team assembled by the president, his leadership, and his money raising capabilities. If you look at those results and recognize, as did the past Board's, his commitment over the many years, rather than other opportunities that could have been open to him, than we should be thankful, not scornful, of the pay package which kept him in the position he held, and still holds."

"I can empathize with Paul Krugman, but the stimulus he's promoting continues to be an uninspiring and misapplication of tax payer money; he'd be putting it in the wrong hands. It should be targeted to promote/advance technologies that address job and wealth creation as well as fashioning a support system that does not take the place of permanent welfare. We need to keep the U.S at the forefront of scientific/technological discovery; so why is it not being given to those who have the best chance of making it happen, and in a way that leverages its return, getting us more bang for our buck. Forget the fat-cats, the major industrial and institutional leaders who no longer get their hands dirty. Put this money to work with the entrepreneurs, the risk takers, the enablers."

"The people who gave us Stimulus I, II and III are still taking bows for spending our money to protect their fellow alumni. The real test, the separation of the men from the boys, is when someone puts his money where his mouth is. I don't see that as a requirement in any round thus far. We need to embrace the Chinese proverb, "No ticky no washy!"

"The Micro-Cap market is the least understood and under-appreciated segment of the stock market in-spite of the fact that it can be mined for outsized gains if one approaches it, not for short term trading profits, but as a small percentage of your long term more conventional and conservative investment portfolio. Micro-Cap investment strategy requires individual commitment, resolve, homework, and a set of guiding principles that one cannot deviate from. Think Peter Lynch and Warren Buffet; not Carl Icahn and Bill Ackman. In following this script, you need to look out 5 to 10 years, as opposed to looking for instant gratification. You also need to think like a VC and private equity analyst in looking for the kind of entrepreneurship and leadership that can build, brick by brick, upon what came before. And don't expect others to applaud; institutional investors and money managers will never spend the time and effort necessary to unearth the opportunities the Micro-Cap market is rife with; your reward will come when they pile on long after you've accumulated your position."

"Micro-Cap investing is more akin to art not science, so you need a palette, not a microscope; no spreadsheets and earnings forecasts, no market timing. Go back and look at many of the recently emerging winners and for the most part you will see that it took time for an entrepreneur and/or a management team to build what the markets eventually deem an overnight success. And I'm not advocating a formula, because there isn't one. The risk factors would fill a book, but you should establish a toolbox, some guidelines, before putting your toe in the water; and I do mean one toe. My suggestion is that you need to make several decisions and distinctions as you winnow out the possibilities. First you need to understand and appreciate what management envisions; what they are trying to build. Ask yourself: What markets are they addressing? Are they large and sustainable and does the company have the wherewithal to penetrate them in a meaningful way over time? Is there a competitive edge because of their innovation, technology, and patents, and do the margins allow for reinvestment without huge dilution to shareholders?

When you identify this, you have an uncut gem that is generally unknown and/or is greatly undervalued, giving you a chance to add more shares to build a meaningful position relative to your investable funds. Typical of these companies is that they quickly achieve cash flow that is immediately reinvested in what now is a formula for growth. Market share is enhanced and new capital will fuel future expansion. Do not focus on earnings; by the time they are predictable it is too late as they will have been extrapolated into price. My advice is that you build a tool box of information; make sure it includes the NY and London Times, WSJ, and as much CNBC Squawk Box as you can assimilate."

"Willie Sutton chose his work space because "that's where the money is"; Sherlock Holmes would add, "It's elementary"; and Burton Malkiel would continue to say that it was no more than "A random walk down Wall Street". My take of it is that if you want to increase your chance of success in seeking Micro Cap winners go where the "best and the brightest" hang out, keep your eyes and ears open, ask a lot of questions, and be aware of what you are looking for. You can get even better advice if you simply get the bible out and reread the encyclicals of Lynch and Buffett.

What you want as an investor is to "discover" early stage companies who are involved in the kind of technology and innovation that can drive outsized growth and profitability over time. Home field for that combination is the intersection where there is a concentration of institutions of higher learning (brains) and capital (brawn). That environment is the foundation from which ten baggers emerge with more regularity than the Pats win super bowls.

You also don't have to be a professional handicapper to appreciate that if you had a choice of casino's you'd spend your time where the slots were programmed at 30/70 rather than 20/80. In going for the home team advantage your choice is obvious; it has to be the Greater Boston area, which we'll define as the city itself, and anywhere you can walk or bike to, as well as connect with, using the ubiquitous MBTA. Did I mention that Harvard, its "B" school, MIT, Babson, BC, BU, Brandeis and Northeastern were still grinding out graduates who never go West. It is the birthplace of venture capital, the mutual fund industry, the family office, and private equity, as well as a world renowned center of medical, biotech, pharma and Big Data research. It's the nirvana of academic and business perfection; which of course is why I'm a stone's throw away from Kendall Square.

For these reasons and for the added pleasure of having easy access to many cultural centers of excellence, there's no lack of opportunity in gaining access to relevant information as well as being able to network for fun and fortune. Almost without exception, if one wants to pursue this diversity of opportunity, you can easily find it at the many either open or relatively inexpensive forums at all of the institutions mentioned above. Tuning in Charlie Rose, CNBC's Squawk Box, the Bloomberg network, and reading what Micro-Cap magazine's founder Shelly

Kraft is expounding, is also rewarding info you can factor into your decision making without having to buy breakfast at the Regency."

"If you want to profit from the Micro-Cap market, as I recommend for 10% of your investible funds, you must do your homework. Get to know those you do bet on, AKA Peter Lynch, who visited parking lots to make sure they were not repositories of Bentleys. Also make sure you are 'recognized" as a player; have calling cards printed with your name, cell and e-mail address, and the phrase "INVESTOR"; you'll be the one gang tackled and forever being pursued and deluged with business plans, "decks", invitations, and new 'best friends'."

"The NYTimes should be applauded for its coverage of the "Opioid Epidemic"; two of many examples being Nicholas Kristof's "How to Win the War on Drugs" (9/24/17), which reported on the way that Portugal treats addiction, i.e., "as a medical problem not a criminal justice issue"; and in "Breaking Opioid Addiction", (10/1/17), which suggested a variety of ways to save addict's lives, as well as the need to inform those in danger.

This is admirable reporting and certainly a far cry from other very important issues of today which 'finger point' rather than educate. However, it does not address, nor is it an answer that helps the largest segment of our addicted population, that of which is composed of the injured and wounded, as well as the older working and retired men and women who have pain so severe, pervasive and persistent, that only opioids can help them. These are not the people who populate our prisons, nor overdose for pleasure. They nevertheless endure many of the same consequences as those who became addicted for other reasons.

President's Obama and Trump, and almost everyone who has expressed deep concern re opioid addiction have pledged to fight this scourge, made it #1 on their agenda, set aside Billions to invest in helping to eradicate it, but have not followed through with grants that truly address the issue. As an example, Massachusetts , in spite of the endorsement of Republican Governor Charley Baker, Democratic minority leader Bruce Tarr, and support from UMass Medical School, a Massachusetts based pharma which has recently filed a patent for a non-addictive alternative to opioids, has had to look to potential investors who ask the same question- 'If it's so good, why hasn't a single dime been spent from Federal funds?'.

I'm sending this letter in hopes it will call attention to our need to identify private citizens and/or institutions that would contact us and do the due diligence that those entrusted to do it, have not. "

"Foxwoods and The Mohegan Sun are licensed and regulated, i.e., subject to oversight, censure, license revocation, and civil and criminal suits. We also claim to be a capitalistic society which means that we punish and reward risk takers, no matter their stripe. We also encourage leverage to increase returns, while at the same time providing protection of principal to those content with a specified return for providing that leverage. And we also operate under "the rule of law", which respects and protects one's "position", which has been clearly spelled out and/or to be determined by the courts.

All this is preamble to the attempt by the Globe ("Betting Against the House"- 2/9/14) to denigrate Foxwoods and The Mohegan Sun for attempting to collect on debt from patrons fully responsible for their own actions. If the Globe truly believes that Casino's that protect their self-interest through due process be punished for allowing bettors to use credit in their wagering, than why are those pols not sponsoring legislation which limits and/or eliminates credit. Our pols understand all too well that this would both lessen taxes collected from the casinos due to gambling and reduce casino jobs. In other words, both the state, local communities and the Casino's knew what they were doing when they gave credit to their bettor's in the first place."

"Just so that I've got this straight; when the decisions were made to shutter Lehman Bros, save the banks, auto manufacturers and a host of other businesses, institutions and anointed beneficiary's that were near and dear to the hearts of our political leaders, and give the Fed the mandate to guide us back to prosperity (a chicken in every pot), there was no claw-back, i.e., a day of summation when the books are audited? Too tough a task; why quibble? While I still would argue that every man for himself would have been a better way to go, it's really pointless and we'd be rehashing this instead of looking back eons from now when we rewrite history."

"Am I wrong, wasn't it all supposed to be about Jobs? If so, we don't have to debate the issue. $800B was spent (equivalent to $10,000 for every homeowner- talk about stimulus and shovel ready construction jobs; or trips to the market, the mall, etc.) and even in high school eco classes we were aware that this equated to a "multiplier effect". However, we did get a predictable stock market lift (very high marks for that), and an eventual fairly significant increase in real estate valuations, all of which were paid for by those people who believed that saving was a virtue, and that you should pay your bills in a timely fashion.

So how about tackling what has already been agreed to is the most important thing we can do is to let the private sector put capital to work (and at risk) in job creation. Under this scenario the chance for commercial success is far more probable. Let's also add another extremely important ingredient. If "We the People" go at risk, we want someone else to suffer if we have to take a loss. It's called 'partnering'. So in moving forward with a QE-4, OUR treasury dollars are matched in any equity investment, start-up, etc. In addition, Our "investment" is conditional upon the following: for all projects valued at less than $100m, We The People receive a 5 yr debt instrument with floating interest tied to treasury bills, a new job has to be created for every $50,000 that we put up (one can make an argument that a new job is created for every investment of at least $35,000- technology companies are generally higher), principals are limited in salary and equity sales until 50% of our money is repaid, and investors (those truly at risk) will receive capital gains tax treatment at the lesser of 20% or their lower marginal rate. And there is a claw-back. If the number of new jobs does not equate to the amount we put up within 6 months, that portion attributable to a new hire, becomes due and payable to us in/within a six month period.

This will require a new governmental agency to set up, supervise, etc. but we already have agencies that can be reconfigured to meet the task. We also know that there will be losses, especially early in the process. However, using monthly treasury inputs that are far below what we are doing now, this will be a "home-run" assuming that 25% will fail within 3 years (but will have gainfully employed 250,000 workers during that period), that 50% will continue with hires during the five years and then begin to repay over the next 5 years, and that 25% of participating businesses will be able to start repayment at the end of the 5 years or sooner. All this is debatable of course, but it seems more reasonable that it will address what is most needed as opposed to the fantasy game now on display."

"My first presidential vote was for Adlai Stevenson. I was an ardent and vocal Kennedy supporter, and voted for Obama for term #1. I cannot recall a single relative who voted for a Republican. I now find myself defending my intended vote for Trump. I also find myself channel surfing each evening to engage in whatever supposed informative discussion is taking place, most of which are an endurance of mind numbing cacophony and biased reporting from those who parade as political experts, rather than the mongers I can only conclude they are. So for my grandkids, and the many who struggle to meet their daily needs while keeping hope eternal, I am "coming out" in an effort to effectuate change for the betterment of my people- the good old U.S of A and the totality of its ethnicity and economic well being; also think the Ten Commandments and The Rule of Law. With that backdrop, and the presumption we're all aboard that express, the answer is obvious. Our #1 priority is creating & keeping jobs here, making sure there is an abundance of educational and employment opportunity, breaking the barriers, either for the individual or the business, that excessive regulation and oversight burden, and just plain 'good sense' when it comes to the treatment and relationship of both enemies and allies. On all of these counts, there should at least be consistency. Let's look at what we'll be getting from either candidate: Hillary- Socialism, more of Obama, open borders, more regulation. Donald- Capitalism, less of Obama, restricted borders, less regulation."

"We're told that Trump is a racist. No one wants one as a president, even though we've had plenty; some/many of which proved to be pretty popular. He may be bombastic, even caustic and self-absorbed at times, but he is not a racist and those that label him one speak with forked tongues. When a guy like Wilbur Ross tells us that he knows Donald very well, is supporting him, and will be part of Donald's inner sanctum that's good enough for me. I only wish that Ken Langone would join the band and take a good look at the man and not the mouth. Donald's not a pol (that should be good enough for everyone) and he kisses no one's rear. Paul Ryan should do what's right for the country never mind The Party. You also know that Donald has a good sense of humor and doesn't pander to the press or that thing above his brow would have been retired. I don't care whether Donald builds The Wall and/or who pays for it. I don't know nor care whether he can make better deals for us with China; or if he becomes a bosom buddy of Putin or doesn't tell us his net worth. We need change and there's a system of checks and balances in place that has worked over the few centuries we've been around. One of the many great things about our country is that we have a chance to make changes every four years. A vote against Trump means that you don't want one now!"

"Let's start with the premise that the one institution that is 'too big to fail' is the U.S. The rest is easy. We go back to The Rule of Law and put everyone on notice- no more 'bail-outs'. The "original sin" took place when Bernanke, Paulson, Rubin and Geithner orchestrated a 'wake' and picked winners instead of punishing the losers by letting them suffer the consequences any other debtor has to deal with. Who would believe it; the perpetrators are all gainfully employed by some of the Wizards of Wall Street. Let's learn from our past mistakes and shit-can quasi corporate government entities, i.e., get rid of the deadwood- reexamine the rules and regulations that have gotten in the way of job growth, and stop tinkering with a free enterprise system, although certainly not perfect, is admired by most. Give me liberty or death, but not water torture."

Ltr. Boston Globe 7/08- "Ross Kerber's interview with Professor Laurence Kotlikoff, "A different take on retirement", and the subtle and disingenuous "Spend to the End" theme, reminds me of the latest diet fad but follow my premise at your own peril. Instead of scratch tickets, Keno, and trips to Vegas and Foxwoods, take 10% of your disposable income and try to find a Highland

Capital Partners fund, or most VC or managed funds, whose portfolio is populated with bridge loans with equity kickers, convertible securities into discounted pending IPO's, or securities of that ilk. In other words, put your 'at risk' money, into the hands of anyone who regularly attends HBS or MIT reunions (that's the extent of your due diligence) and look for home runs rather than getting hit by a pitched ball to get to first. The problem with this approach is in finding such a vehicle. The regulators (SEC, FINRA, State's Attorney Generals, etc.) don't want us swimming in the rapids; that's reserved for Accredited Investors, not working stiffs. My guess is that Wall Street will soon wake up to this oversight and create a new pool for 'the fish' to swim in. After all, with a dearth of new products and their income negatively impacted by low interest rates, cash being sequestered in piggy banks, little if any stock tips from taxi drivers, the financial services industry (brokers who summer in Nantucket and the Hamptons) need new blood. What better way than to put some holy water on SPECULATION and allow more drilling off the coast of Florida?"

Ltr. WSJ 12/22/08- "Washington is Killing Silicon Valley" ("Opinion" by Michael Malone), is on point but doesn't mention many of the other culprits, i.e., the investment banking giants who took leadership roles on every meaningful regulatory committee to insure they could shuffle the deck and deal the kind of hands that would protect their turf. Ditto for the holy water dispensers of fact and fiction, our Big 8 (then 7, 6, 5 and 4). These so called accounting mavens, elbowed their way to their own space at the trough, making sure that they could high-jack every entity, no matter the weight-class, and insure there was more paperwork and upfront payment for their blessing. The SEC has also lost its way, i.e., forgot what crucial role those in the small cap arena meant to our country, and are beating up on those waiting in the wings to add jobs and taxes to a faltering champ, the Good-Old-U.S of A.

On this latter score, just ask any securities attorney who deals with this burden every day. The SEC believes that it knows what is best for all of us, and act as Roman emperor's, giving their own version of thumbs up or down. The results of these and other inequities has been to place insurmountable obstacles in the path of the early stage and start-up companies that were our job and growth creators."

My Commandments
- Be unwavering in the face of criticism and disbelief.
- Be aware of the possibility of self-deception; question your direction as you continuously data-mine for additional information.
- Impose your will; but tend to the needs of your teammates.

-         Know when to turn off the lights, where to get another torch, and/or recharge.

Ltr. NYTimes 12-08- "Tom Friedman has gone to the play numerous times and according to him "It always ends badly" ("Win, Win, Win"). That's because Tom believes that throwing money at renewable energy projects will ultimately be in our best interest. My guess is that he would be correct if the money used from his proposed gas tax (wonder what that proposal would ultimately look like?) would be spent solely for that purpose; which of course is a fairy tale. Another Friedman assumption is that these extra tax dollars, are more burdensome to the already downtrodden, and would be doled out to the appropriate companies/people- we've all been to That play, and continually ask Mrs. Lincoln what she thought about it."

"I don't hear Boone Pickens or Larry Kudlow saying "Drill" "Drill" "Drill" anymore. Of course, they will be back, as will the markets; and somehow, somewhere, in the best tradition of capitalism, and against all the odds foisted upon us by the regulators (read-SEC, FINRA, SOX advocates, etc.), companies, not politicians, will create the products and services we need to recharge our self-inflicted sputtering economy. The script for Tom's play cannot be written by Tom or our present leadership. They may believe they can make a stab at it, but they cannot overcome the mountains of red tape, political infighting, self interest groups, and pontificators who only know what is good for everyone else. Let's go to work, respect one another, and have peace and good will in our hearts. If we truly believe in our system, let's allow it to work. The play may change but the theatre remains the same. "

Ltr. Financial Times 4/20/09- "There are many reasons, opinions, explanations, alibis, rationalizations as to the "Why?" for the collapse of the VC model (Financial Times, 4/20/09; Venture Capital Investment Falls). The most obvious to me, but one that is rarely mentioned, is that the VC community relied on their B School buddies in the investment banks/brokerage houses to bail them out (hyping their returns and hence their place in the sun) by overpricing their deals at the IPO level and allowing them to either sell out at preposterous valuations and/or use these mark-to-the-market levels to coral additional fund investors. In other words, leave some crumbs on the table for run of the mill as well as professional (institutional, family offices) investors. Notwithstanding the foregoing, we need the VC community now more than ever. They fund the entrepreneurs that will extract us from the mess that the financial gurus at our tiller have saddled us with. These entrepreneurial activities create the jobs and enterprises that result from their expertise, laborious work, and unbounded faith in their own ability to perform. What our regulators have to do is get a dose of reality and accept the fact that they and their legislative kin, have to go back to the system that gave us relatively free and open markets with appropriate safeguards which also allowed our micro-cap's fair access to a broad spectrum of possible investors, instead of having to seek handouts from the favored few."

Ltr. NYTimes 1/1/12- "How can one escape the irony of Devon Leonards's "After a Year of Tumult, former Bailout Chief Took a Quiet Path to Pimpco" (NYT's 1/1/10), when you reflect on the Rajarajnam/Galleon case and the squid-like tentacles of Goldman. Do you think that our regulators are asking the powers at Pimco for e-mails, telephone records, and meetings with Neel Kashkari, and then comparing the timing with portfolio buys and sells?"

"Wall Street devours its own. He who has the Gold dictates. You either live and survive and thrive by this dictum or best head for the showers. So in accepting these two maxims, it's a relatively even playing field, plenty of hits and piling on, and a mutual understanding and respect for power. On the other hand there is a new sheriff in town; or a dictator if you will. It's the SEC. While pledged to insure protection for both the weak and the mighty (leave out for a moment the "Public", both you and I, and think of the combatants), they consistently hammer the weak, without any hint of compassion. As "umps" they're homers for those in the bulge bracket firms. They're also totally and shamelessly biased versus start-ups and early stage small caps, while also dumping on what they consider the minor league community of securities dealers, attorneys, accountants, and IR professionals that toil in this space. The classic IPO has been high jacked, disemboweled and burdened (buried) so that the unaccredited (unsophisticated would be their lingo) are free to buy more lottery and scratch tickets."

Ltr. Wall Street Journal 6/30/12- "The Wall Street Journal should be commended for extolling the potential virtues of Crowd Funding. Small investors (defined as "unaccredited", labeled as "unsophisticated"), can now employ this "alternative investment" vehicle to get odds much more in their favor as opposed to the lottery and scratch ticket option sponsored by our pol's as veiled taxing measures (SHAME!). These new investors (no matter how shallow their pockets) now have a chance to enjoy the action, and possibly get a liquidity event in which they can elect their own taxing alternatives as opposed to expropriation upon distribution. What will Mary Schapiro say about all of this? .... Depending on her decision, we may have another Wall Street sit-in!"

Ltr. NYTimes 7/12- "A suggestion for Andrew Ross Sorkin in light of his Sean Parker interview (Deal Book and VC Observations) – Andrew, once you take money from the Pro's (VC/Private Equity), you are no longer a virgin nor an entrepreneur. Sean opted for what he thought would be a safety net and a real life. Chances are he's made a poor choice. Suggest you call him in a year and see if his expectations were met."

Ltr. NYTimes 4/12- "After I read E. L. Doctorow's musings, I knew why I continued my monthly subscription, even though your extraordinary editorial bias re the upcoming presidential race was comical enough to draw a few laughs from me. The fact is that if one fails to read periodicals favored by the non-mainstream media, you will miss some extraordinary brilliance. For this reason, and your Sunday edition, I will continue to look forward to the continuing of our relationship. Doctorow's thought provoking sentiments, and others of that ilk, are difficult to encounter elsewhere unless you had the time, energy and resources to mine the Library of Congress."

Ltr. Wall Street Journal 4/11-"It's not my opinion, nor was it Stephen Moore's (We've become a Nation of Takers, Not Makers), that everyone who works for the government isn't doing a good job and/or is overpaid. It's simply that the rest of us cannot afford their cost. While I could point to numerous inefficiencies and inequities that our bureaucratic infrastructure imposes, the most burdensome is the frustration and waste inflicted by our regulators. The problem is that they think they have to do something to justify their existence, and that translates into imposing their will or bias, delivered via a "them versus us" mentality."

Ltr NY Times 6/13-"What legal premise am I missing that presumes that Steven Cohen (SAC Capital Advisors) and Jon Corzine (MF Global) are responsible for the criminal acts of those working for them? Apparently the Fed's cannot make a case of collusion, fraud, or "What-Ever ?". Unless Cohen or Corzine embraced a company playbook that promoted illegal behavior and the evidence overwhelmingly substantiates it, we'll soon see a stampede to the Supreme Court which will set a new Olympic record."

Ltr. NY Times 2/13-"Gretchen Morgenson's columns are generally about accountability; so why doesn't she name names? Instead of referring to the NY Fed, give us the names of those members alluded to, and their past and present additional affiliations; we can then try and figure out the "why's" of their positions. On the other hand, in a neighboring column, Frank Bruni doesn't talk about "the new Tea Party Senator from Texas dumping on Chuck Hagel; he identifies Ted Cruz as the assailant, putting a face on the culprit. Come to think about it; that's why more reporters and politicians should wear body cameras with rear-view mirrors."

"I know the difference between a socialist and capitalist and/or those that go down either path. For me either bias is much less important in getting my vote than my assumptions (guess) as to the people a candidate chooses to have on his team, and in that candidate's ability to follow through and execute whatever their advice. I could live, and I believe we as a nation would prosper, with any of the candidates; it's their "team" that I have reservations about. This is not a "Give me liberty or give me death" moment for us as a nation, or is it?"

Ltr. Boston Globe 2/15 "Let me make sure that I've got this right. Ted Cutler, a Bostonian, a self-made philanthropist who pays taxes and is not asking for any special favors, is independently supporting and managing a city-wide event of obvious benefit to the community, is being faulted in the press for philanthropy. Shame on those who would like to micro-manage a well-intentioned and magnificent gift because they weren't asked for either their opinion, help, or participation. Ted wants to make sure that the results of his efforts reflect his vision. No wonder few like Ted step to the plate when their efforts often result in what's encountered in this act of generosity."

Ltr. Barron's Mailbag 8/13 "When the decision was made to shutter Lehman, rescue the banks, auto manufacturers, and a host of other 'too big to fail' beneficiaries so we could strive for Roosevelt's "Chicken in every Pot", there was no provision for a future audit. While I would posit that the law of the land - 'every man for himself', would have been a better way to go, it is pointless to spend time debating it now. Let's focus on examining QE3, which we were led to believe was all about JOBS. If so, the answer is in. $800B was spent without any real indication of success (job creation), except for the very predictable stock market elevation and the increase in real estate valuations, most of which was essentially paid for by those who believed that saving was a virtue and that you pay bills, work as much as you can, and reduce debt before it is due."

Ltr. Barron's- "Jim Mcguire's Fix DC is on the mark and will be the subject for debate for years to come. For me, a simpler and far more effective alternative would have been to recognize that the private sector has always been far more successful in putting money to work in creating and maintaining jobs than the public sector, with few exceptions. Personal accountability tied to rewarding success trumps whatever else is out there, what our capitalistic system is all about, and what will eventually give us more of the same."

"Let's have a QE4 that matches, dollar for dollar, any new equity investment, whether start-up or ongoing phase, conditional upon the following; a) participating companies have valuations of $100M or less, b) the investment is structured as a five year debt instrument with floating interest accruing quarterly at a 1% rate above treasury bills, c) a new job must be created during the ensuing 6 month period for every $50k of investment or the $50k is due and payable in/within the next 6 month period or the borrower is in default, d) principals of those businesses are limited in both salary and personal equity sales until 50% of borrowed Fed funds are repaid, and e) new equity investors during that period receive tax benefits on sale at the lesser of 20% of the gain or their lower marginal rate. As for administration of QE4, we have agencies that can be reconfigured to meet the administrative task. We can expect early losses but the odds are that this approach will be a home-run for us, even putting up a mere $100B/month and assuming that 25% of participants default in/within three years, having in fact gainfully employed 250,000 workers during that period. We can most likely expect 50% of the businesses to repay over the next 5 years, and only 25% start repayment after the fifth year. Although these results can be defended based on a lot of text book data, reality is the only true test, but there is a real probability of success, somewhat limited and off the mark (perhaps?), but its probability is closer to fact, and a better way to go, as opposed to the fantasy games being played today."

"Trump is an enigma to most of the media. They're used to being fawned over by candidates that need them to reciprocate via implied endorsement. Our so called 'pundits' think they are more "intelligent" and understanding and do a better job than any of the candidates anyway. Trump, to their chagrin won't allow it. Most reach out for a "gotcha" moment, generally for their own celebrity and perverted self-esteem. They consistently remind us that Trump is a billionaire, as if that was a failing and infectious disease. You don't hear Donald labeling them as pimps, a more telling statement about their intent, especially when you couple that with their employer's proclivities. I'm waiting for one of these psychopaths to tell me why their candidate of choice should be voted for in spite of all the warts and weaknesses that are apparent in each of the others in this campaign. Sad to say, I don't see any of them playing on my Field of Dreams."

Ltr. NYT's 7/16 "I took Andrew Ross Sorkin's advice and read Mohamed A. El-Erian's "The Only Game In Town". Brilliantly written but prejudicial in both his examination and explanation of the 'bail-out' and the ensuing Fed handling of the 2008 economic meltdown and stock market crash. Unfortunately for most Americans, the title of Mohamed's book says it all. The architects, Hank Paulson, Ben Bernanke, Bob Rubin, Larry Summers and Tim Geithner (all now gainfully employed or tied to the umbilical cord of the Wall Street Crowd) had other options but opted for a game that only a few could play, which ultimately resulted in a path that a preponderance of our citizenry is now struggling to recover from.

Mohamed's new normal of low growth, rising inequality, political dysfunction and in some cases social tensions – all despite massive policy interventions on the part of central banks", suggests that he still hasn't figured it out: It isn't "despite of", it's "because of" ; what we needed was an enema not a banquet."

CHAPTER 8

Some of my tweets (@GodfatherofURBN)

"Harvard B school's poster boy (Uber) has yet another black eye. Looks like their Case Study has become the Ostrich in a room of Unicorns."

"What Trump did with climate initiatives was to foster, not to crush. Our so called business elite have little idea of what drives innovation."

"We aren't "abandoning" climate initiatives. We ARE retaking control of our own destiny. Let's start the discussion, not shoot the messenger."

"Not only is there an opioid crisis, but everyone seems to be on steroids; "voice matters"! What happened to Reason and Common Sense?"

Being civil? -it died! And its loss is painful. The 'voices' are not of reason. Wherefore are they if not in the NY Times or college campuses?"

"Where are the censors @ NYTimes? In Economic View- "Workers are capturing more than their share of a growing economy". Truth is no fiction!"

"My breakfast with Atty Jan Schlichtmann an education in 3 Principals of our judicial system: POWER, LAW and JUSTICE. Keep it in mind!

"Someone just called me an "old goat". Exhilarating and true. I've been "unmasked".

"Corzine's wife quoted in NYTimes: "It's not risk to him. It's conviction." She's defining all entrepreneurs and hedge fund managers."

"Not even considering RISK is like saying "No" to Opportunity. Don't waste our time if this applies to you."

"Looney Tunes"- Media Mavens comparing/equating Trump to Nixon. No longer reporters, they're now cartoonists."

"A Sam Zell-ion- "Always make sure you're getting paid for the risk you take and never risk what you cannot afford to lose."

Bret Stephen's in NYTimes today- "We are protected, for the time being, by the President's stupidity"- Nothing's Sacred!"

"Sam Zell- Read his book. No forked tongue; willing to use an open mind in considering opportunities and relationships. How unique in today's world."

"Too few do not understand/accept/appreciate "Due "Process". In my world excuses fall on deaf ears. "Reality" challenges all of us. Go for i!"

"Excuses? irrational fabrication. When does an individual take responsibility for their own circumstance? We don't see much of it."

"Free speech is not equated to honest journalism. It's been missing and unfortunately most cannot tell the difference."

"HBS is in the grip of an administration and faculty that is compromised and flawed- succumbed by Uber fever. Where's our Alumni? Anyone?

"Tom Friedman and his buddies at the NYTimes are prejudiced & programmed to influence the Herd, versus those of us who embrace capitalism."

"NY Times' Kristoff forgot his 8/28/11 appeal- "Mr. Obama, with 25m American's hurting, will you fight to put jobs on top of agenda?". Donald did!

"It's easy to be a cynic and a critic. Instead, work to make something of substance happen or get out of the way. Responsibility matters. Take it!"

"NYTimes Tom Friedman continues to lose credibility by belaying our president's inclusiveness. Consider T's appointments vs. the past administrations."

"Self Interest is not a bad thing; in fact, it's pervasive. Recognize it; use it; profit by it; help others."

"WSJ Opinion"- "The Price of Obama's Mendacity"- as in, Not Truthful, Lying, Falsehood (see Webster's). We need/want Fact not Fiction. Go USA!"

"Be thankful for what you get/have. Be responsible for your actions thereafter. "Free meals" are for the downtrodden and infirm, Work Works!

"Relentless, Focused, Driven, Undaunted- the characteristics of those who make their own luck. Let's hope these attributes become endemic once again."

"Moore's Law is essentially about information: the ability to access, accumulate, store, retrieve, and disseminate. Talk about opportunity! Get in line."

"RIP Gershon Kekst. He offered others "saykhl"- common sense/judgment. Wilbur Ross is his 2nd incantation."

"While it's often forgotten, we're reminded daily that the primary rule in selling is to appeal to what's in the "best interest" of the buyer. Get this message to our Pols."

"Today's pundits have a premise and try to prove their point instead of seeking "truth" by starting with a blank sheet an building their case on facts."

"Ideologues cannot be won over by love, aid and acts of kindness. One needs to eradicate the disease, not extend its life."

"Tom Friedman's "Thank You For Being Late" makes the best case for our Pres. Tom needs to listen to himself, not his employer."

"In the real world "judgment" comes from the capital markets. Anyone who thinks and talks otherwise is making a fraudulent case for their own beliefs- "Forked Tongues".

"We need to explain to our kids and their teachers the difference between "incite"- to set in motion/stir-up, and "insight"-the ability to see/understand."

"David Tepper on Squawk Box: "There's a time to make money in the stock market and a time not to lose $." Not bad advice, but it would be great if Tepper would tell us what time it really is."

"Looking forward to CNBC Squawk Box 20th anniversary week. Becky, Joe Thank You!"

"One of the most important words of advice: "LISTEN"

"I want to go 'OUT' on the playing field, not in the grandstand."

"Lose my Tweets if you don't agree with me that John Leferve's "Straight to Hell" is a tail you cannot put down."

"Kiss Ass Comment: Mohammed El-Elarian gives Fed a free pass by saying they were experimenting."

"Coming soon to the Guinness Record Book: The shortest lived species on the planet- the Unicorn. Food ran out and none could farm."

"Don't lead the life you aspire to; embrace and enjoy the one you can afford"

"If $ equates to a good life, and business induces proclivity, it is only natural that egregious self-interest has to be pervasive."

"Equality and Equal Opportunity should not be viewed as an "entitlement", but as "entitled to"."

"Make something happen. Leadership is recognized, valued and rewarded."

"Deserving"? That's the core of the debate until election-day. My suggestion is that all candidates set forth and sign a pledge."

Frank Bruni, NYTimes- "Public service is a fig leaf over private cupidity. A prelude to a lucrative payday they (politicians) are counting on."

"Success? - Feeling good about yourself. Otherwise keep trucken".

"An open, inquiring, probing mind by our "leadership" is what we need if we are to lift all boats. If it was ever there, how about a return to humanity?"

"Insidious and repugnant behavior is the perpetration of a lie by government agencies against one of its citizens."

"Play the hand you're dealt without complaint; improve your game and chances are you'll make your mark"

"Never forget where you came from and what it took to get where you are today; that the truest test of character."

"Ray Dirks should be deified by attorneys who practice the "Rule of Law" versus their SEC counterparts."

"Time flies; follow your gut, appreciate that "character" marks the individual. Legacy is what's life's about. Don't squander that opportunity."

"Regulatory Capture; ceding control to those they oversee; it's the Revolving Door and One Hand Washes another syndrome that has infected Washington."

"It's one thing to "self-destruct"; take it like a man. However if inflicted by a Predator or Informer, inflict your own pain"

"The Economy? No crystal balls; it's always a question of when and who pay the piper."

"Once you acknowledge that "self-interest" drives decision making, you'll appreciate why politicians cannot "rise above".

"Not everyone is created equal; but everyone should have the opportunity to more than make up for that difference."

"Reality check: Is it all about YOU, or do you really want to make a difference?"

"Today I'm thinking: Follow "The Impossible Dream." For those who would succumb to this, be prepared to change course."

"Social media has now provided anyone with a mouth a "voice".

"Logic is useful, but don't use it as an excuse not to travel down some less used paths."

"Bite off more than you can chew and then finish the meal. Do the extra lap no matter the obstacles and the unanticipated consequences."

"VACANT"; is there a more bleak condition? These signs are all over D.C."

"Better to implement a plan and set sail rather than continue to look for the perfect route. Just be prepared to change course and man the oars."

"Every day is a blessing. Honor it through commitment to 'character' and helping those less fortunate."

"Beauty is skin deep; the mind is deep-less and the Soul has no borders. Where is your life anchored?"

"The difference between Eric Cantor and a suicide bomber is that the bomber kills the enemy."

"Our Fed has turned the nation's balance sheet into garbage" (Jim Rogers) "Our challenge is to recycle it without creating inflation." (Marshall Sterman)

"Well rounded is out; specialization is in. Do you think the misfits should get their Ivy League tuition back?"

"Parent pays double tuition; kid gets into school and a one full year scholarship for a deserving student is funded. Why isn't it worth a trial, and who's the better bet to help endow the school in the future? I think it's a coin toss."

"The Almighty has a first lien on all your assets. What legacy will you leave?"

"SAC's Steinberg gets 3.5 years while GM execs who killed and maimed get retirement payments. Who's kidding whom? Justice IS blind!"

"Frustration means that you have to change/rethink your strategy. It's you that doesn't get it."

"Tim Geithner: nice guy; tried his best; honest, honorable. Stooge for Robert Rubin. Tragic for the country."

"To college students no matter color, ethnicity, economic standing; you are all there because of "privilege". Don't throw stones."

"Wisdom: When one abandons their 'wish list' and takes what they can get."

"Stock buybacks similar to Fed's stimulus- neither creates jobs." "Think/Consider your idea: Possible? Plausible? Reasonable? Certain! ACT-Make it happen!"

"I recognize that one size doesn't fit all but if you want to be an entrepreneur get a job 1st. You owe it to your life."

High Frequency Trading? Electronic front-running? If the SEC doesn't care, it becomes yesterday's news."

"Life's test: A. Trust/Character; B. Truth/Honesty"

"Relationships- Treasure and continue no matter how fragile. The pendulum swings; times change. There's another tomorrow."

"Wall Street is one way. We need to create a two-way street so that others can benefit."

"No offence intended: Make it your #1 priority be responsible for your actions."

"Athletes as employees? The beginning of the end of college athletics."

"Data is dumb, but dangerous in its interpretation, use and protection. Beware the know-it-all's."

"Advice to the US, Russia and European Union: People in glass houses should not throw rocks."

"Shadow Banks? Thanks to Bernanke and our Too Big to Fail (bailed out) Bankers. At least their doors are open to those in need."

"There is no more satisfaction than having a positive impact on the lives of others."

"Prepare to be a 'player' in life. Get out of the grandstand and to the plate. Positive attitude is a necessary attribute. Dress up for the Game. "

"Motivation creates energy, but it's only the fuel, the starter, not the steering wheel. Be relentless in pursuing your objective."

"We better get our act together. Even Russia is planning to eliminate capital gains taxes for early stage, innovative companies looking for capital."
"July 4th Pronouncement: Due Process has been high jacked by those entrusted to defend and honor it. Who is the criminal?"

"Diversity is not a synonym for equality, nor for opportunity.; it's a journey where obstacles should be identified and eliminated."

"Donald will figure out where the S. China Sea is before Hillary can negotiate a deal." CNBC's Joe Kernen

"The more excuses I hear about the lack of job creation the more I'm for flushing the toilet that holds the huge DC cesspool."

"Northeastern Professor Alexander Gorlov funeral was today. Truly a remarkable individual, whose intellect, daring, humility and kindness were unparalleled."

"Advice to supporters: From Donald- Keep repeating "Sticks and Stones". From Hillary- "I overcharged and under-delivered for my paid Wall Street speeches"."

"Reminder to NYTimes: "Imprecise" is the language of Politicians and Rogues. All our candidates speak with "forked tongues"."

"US #1 priority: Creating & keeping jobs here. Who would you bet on for this- Hillary or Donald?"

"On CNBC Squawk Box Joe K eviscerates GOP political consultant. What 'establishment'? We need change!"

"The message in my fortune cookie tonight; "A mentor is someone whose hindsight can become your foresight."

"Let's do something about 'intolerant behavior', no matter where found- that includes US govt agencies and their employees; all lives matter!"

"Query: Will a Whistleblower Suit vs. a govt. agency be acknowledged/recognized & if successful, who pays?"

"LEADERSHIP-"assertion to fill a void"; manifested by the person that steps to the plate no matter the next designated hitter."

"If the world had a referee he would call "time out", penalize all players and coaches, watch a replay, and end the sea   "Blame is often a fiction; we put a face to it because there is no logical conclusion for failure. Fame and Fortune are not a given."

"Certainly a consideration: Whom among our candidates used their own $ (were at risk personally) to create jobs?"

"New Year's Thought: What you know doesn't matter: It's what you do with it! If you think it's good, make it happen."

"Prejudicial wordsmithing by the NY Times re Sheldon Adelson's newspaper acquisition: Why not "Strategic Acquisition" versus "Power Play?"

"This week on Wall Street: Rationalization – a lot of $$ managers making cases for something they got wrong."

"No need to seek an explanation. Accept reality; build something of value from what exists!"

"There is no more satisfaction than having a positive impact on the lives of others"

"Prepare yourself to be a "player". Get to the plate and out of the grandstand. Positive attitude is an attribute. Dress up for the Game!"